by Chana Mason

For my mom, Lucy Gateño,
for believing in me even when I didn't.

Foreword

Here's the good news: we are all, yourself included, innately whole and healthy. Sometimes there's a barrier stifling our natural vibrancy and mental clarity. More often than not, what's holding us back is a thought or belief. Through Inquiry, a process of asking truth-seeking questions, we can zoom out and question our beliefs and the suffering they cause. Once we identify a given thought, disentangle our mind from it, and observe it from the outside, we can find our way back to ourselves.

Most of our beliefs live in the submerged bulk of our subconscious mind. The focus of Inquiry is to flash as bright a light on that bulk as possible, question the veracity of our thinking, and chose beliefs that bring us more clarity and joy. In this book, I'll share tools that enhance this light. You can use them to facilitate your own Inquiries with a notebook in hand, in processing your thoughts with a friend, or in a therapeutic setting as a coach or counselor.

In the first section of this book, ***Thought Collection***, we'll explore tools to identify the thoughts causing our distress. In the second section, ***Words to Suffer By***, we'll shine a light on the language patterns that lead us down dark alleyways of consciousness. The third section, ***Reaction Contraction***, will help us understand our reactions to our thinking and how those reactions can lead to even more destructive beliefs. In the fourth section, **A Fresh Pair of Lenses**, we'll explore how our limiting beliefs conceal lessons that can help us become better human beings.

The dialogues in this book are either approximated transcripts or piecemeal collection of actual conversations with clients. All names and identifying characteristics have been changed to protect their privacy.

I've had workshop participants with advanced degrees in psychology balk at the simplicity of Inquiry—it's hard for them to imagine that their clients can find healing from a handful of simple questions—but I've seen clients dealing with everything from panic attacks to eating disorders find peace and light-heartedness just by questioning their thinking.

I bless you to trust that everything we need to find happiness is already within us. By asking questions, we create a space for gems of understanding to bubble up to the surface, leading us toward understanding, compassion, peace, and joy.

If you have benefited from any of the teachings shared in this book, or if you have tools or insights of your own, I would *love* to hear from you.

Wishing you many joys,
Chana Mason
Jerusalem, Israel

Visit my site at **ChanaMason.com**
You can email me at **ChanaMason@gmail.com**

A TASTE OF INQUIRY

*My first thought was always a cigarette.
It still is, but I haven't cheated.*

Frederik Pohl

"I don't get this Inquiry thing," I told my friend, Noga. "Why would I want to change my mind about something that is absolutely true?"

"What do you mean?" she asked.

About an hour before, I was standing at a bus stop waiting for my 5-year-old to arrive on his bus home from kindergarten. A few others were also at the stop, but I only paid attention to one of them: a guy in his 20s wearing brown pants, a loose shirt, and headphones. He was smoking a cigarette. Right there, at *my* bus stop. The nerve!

I stared at this guy and seethed. How could he stand next to a whole bunch of people and smoke like that? How could he infest us all with his second-hand poison? Didn't he know about the Surgeon General's warning? Didn't he know how bad smoking was for him?

If I were a cartoon character, smoke would've been billowing out of my ears, and the top of my head would've shot up like the lid of a pressure cooker. As soon as my son got off his bus, we dashed home, and I stomped over to Noga's.

"So," she asked, "What do you believe about the situation that got you so angry?"

"What do you mean, what do I *believe*? The guy was smoking. It was so disgusting!"

"So you think he shouldn't have been smoking?"

"Yes, exactly."

"There you go. You believe he shouldn't smoke. That's why you're all upset."

"But he shouldn't smoke," I huffed. "That's just a fact. Do you have any idea how many studies have been done showing the connection between cigarettes and cancer, heart disease, not to mention emphysema? And -"

"What you're telling me is that you have a lot of reasons to believe your story that he shouldn't smoke."

"Tons."

"But what's the reality of it?"

I suddenly stopped in my tracks. "What do you mean?"

"What does the man *actually* do?"

7

"Oh. He smokes."

Noga smiled. "Yes."

"I don't get it."

"Why don't we do *The Work* on this thought, and see if you can gain some clarity."

Noga had recently given me *Loving What Is* by Byron Katie. I'd already read a bunch of Barry Neil Kaufman's works and was drawn to the premise that thoughts shape our world, but I hadn't internalized any of it. Not only that, I fought the idea of Inquiry like a Jerusalem cat in a turf war. There were so many things to argue about: How could my thoughts possibly not *be me*? How could something not be true if it *feels* so true? How was I supposed to *not worry* about things; wouldn't that mean I didn't care? Fortunately for me, my friend was patient.

In the chapters ahead, I'll expound on every question and tool you see below. For now, enjoy the ride.

Noga: He shouldn't smoke - Is it true?

This is the first question in Byron Katie's four question process, *The Work*.

Chana: Yes!

Noga: Can you absolutely know it's true that he shouldn't smoke?

Chana: Need I mention the science again?

Noga: I'll take that as a yes. And how do you react when you believe the thought?

Chana: I get outraged. My fists ball up. My chest gets tight.

Noga: What are you unable to do when you believe the thought?

Chana: I can't think straight. I can't... oh my gosh! (I slapped my forehead.) I just stood there breathing the smoke. I could have moved away or asked him to stop, but I didn't. When I believe the thought I can't take care of myself at all.

Noga: So whose business are you in when you believe he shouldn't smoke?

Chana: Huh?

Noga: Were you focusing on what you can control or what he controls?

Chana: Oh. Okay. I was in his business. I can't control whether he smokes or not.

Noga: That's why you stood still. When you left yourself to meddle in his business, there was no one left to take care of you. Now we get to the last question. Take a deep breathe and imagine yourself at the bus stop. How would you be without the thought?

Chana: I'd be calmer. Just waiting for my son. I'd probably walk further away and then I wouldn't have to breathe the smoke

Noga: Good. Now let's turn it around. What's the opposite of he shouldn't smoke?

Chana: He should smoke? But that's insane! I can't believe that - it's so unhealthy to smoke.

Noga: Why don't you try and see if you can find a reason why it might be true?

Chana: I can't. Help me out here.

Noga: Okay. How about, maybe if he didn't smoke, he might use a more dangerous drug or alcohol?

Chana: I never thought of that. Maybe he's gone through difficult stuff, and smoking helps him cope.

Noga: Exactly. Can you give me another reason?

Chana: Maybe he's so addicted that it's hard to stop?

Noga: One more…

Chana: Maybe he doesn't care that it's bad for him. Maybe he likes it.

That thought made me cringe, but I had to admit I knew smokers who loved their cigarettes more than anything.

Noga: Fantastic! You got three right there. What's another turnaround? Try changing the subject this time.

Chana: I shouldn't smoke? But I don't.

Noga: And that's one reason why you shouldn't: because it's not the reality. Can you give me more?

Chana: I can't stand the smell. And smoke it makes me cough.

Noga: We could also be more creative on this one. It seems to me, that in this situation you were smoking plenty.

Chana: Me? How?

Noga: You told me you got so angry, smoke came out of your ears.

Chana: Oh, yeah.

Noga: And even though he's long gone, you're still thinking about him. For all we know, he hasn't smoked the rest of the day -

Chana: But he's chain-smoking in my head.

Noga: Exactly. And there are other things you use the way this man uses cigarettes…

Chana: (I bit my lip.) Like my phone or staying up late… or chocolate.

Noga: Maybe he's there to teach you about your addictions. You can't fix him, but perhaps you can stop the phone, late night, or chocolate addictions you have.

Chana: That's so hard.

Noga: You thought it was so easy for him. (We both laughed.)

Chana: Got it. So he should smoke and I… I should work on not smoking - not him, not my addictions, not my anger.

Noga: And when you've got that down, you can teach me how you did it.

Chana: I don't know if I ever will

Noga: Neither does he. Really, you're the same.

Chana: I guess I could have more compassion for him.

Noga: That might be a kinder way to live.

That conversation was a turning point in my life. For the first time, I got a taste of how powerful it can be to question my thinking. I've been hooked ever since.

Gleaning Thoughts:
IDENTIFYING YOUR SUFFERING

*We are addicted to our thoughts.
We cannot change anything if we
cannot change our thinking*

Santosh Kalwar

If you're like many of my clients, you sometimes find yourself feeling yucky, but not knowing exactly why. You might be able to pin down your frustration to a specific person or situation but are unclear as to what thoughts are leading you down a rabbit hole. Hopefully, by now, you've come to understand (though perhaps not fully live out) the truth that it is our response to life, our story about it, and not our circumstance that causes our suffering. Once you can identify the thoughts constructing your narrative, you can pull them apart, inspect them, keep what serves you, and chuck or rework what's hurting you.

The key to working on our thoughts is nailing down exactly what they are. In this section, we'll cover a collection of tools to help you glean the beliefs you have about a given situation or person; dig deep into uncovering your most hidden thoughts about yourself, life, and all that is sacred; and identify the ones you can work on to create the most significant shift in your emotional experience.

The Rant

A tool for gathering overt or implied thoughts expressed by a speaker's stream of consciousness.

As you think, so shall you be.

- Wayne Dyer

People often don't know what exactly is blocking them from moving forward. They might not know how to identify their thinking or are scared of the thoughts swimming under the surface. This might lead to some very "blah" dialogues. Warning: if you try to work on a blah thought, you'll get blah results. **The Rant** is an excellent tool for identifying the bigger issues beneath.

Jane walked into my office unable to settle down enough to sit. She teetered from one foot to the other as she answered my "How are you doing?" with, "I dunno."

Chana: What do you mean when you say, "You don't know?"

Jane: Just that, I feel upset, sort of. Well, not exactly upset… more like, frustrated.

Chana: So you're frustrated. What about?

Jane: I don't think frustrated is the word. It's more like – uneasy.

Jane has a collection of emotions she's struggling to identify, and she's jumping from one to the next. We can keep playing pin the tail on the feeling or move on to what I consider to be a more useful exercise: pin the tail on the thoughts.

A core principle of Inquiry is that every emotion is triggered by a thought. For Jane, experiencing a collection of painful feelings means she's believing a whole stew of painful thoughts. Recognizing these thoughts is the most useful next step:

Chana: What thoughts are causing you upset right now?

Jane: I'm not sure. I'm just annoyed at my sister. Something happened yesterday.

Jane doesn't know on a conscious level what specific *thoughts* are causing her upset; rather there's a whole *story* fueling her feelings, and that story has a slew of beliefs at its foundation. By hearing the story, I can use my outsider's perspective to identify these thoughts and reflect them back to Jane.

I invited Jane to **Rant** and pulled out all the thoughts she overtly stated and the ones I could hear between the lines. **Ranting** gave Jane the opportunity to talk freely without having to filter her words or cognitively understand her every motive. You'll see Jane's story on the left. Cover the **Thought Bank** I formulated on the right, and write down what thoughts you guess Jane believed as she told her story. (We'll delve into the concept of a **Thought Bank** in a couple of chapters. For now, it's enough for you to know it's a collection of thoughts or beliefs.) Once you've done so, take a look at my collection.

Jane's Story	Thought Bank
Katlyn came to visit yesterday. The minute she walked in the door, she started picking up the kids' toys and putting them in the toy chest. Then she walked into my kitchen and washed the dishes. She didn't even ask me if I wanted her to do these things. It made me feel so uncomfortable - like she just thinks I'm a slob. We sat down for lunch, and while I was still telling her about Johnny's fight with his baseball coach, she picked up the plates and took them into the kitchen. It's like she's my mom or something. She doesn't think I can look after myself. Her kids are all grown, so now she has to mother me. It's so embarrassing. Why can't she just believe in me? She doesn't even trust I can take care of my kids. She asked me if I wanted her to go to Johnny's next ballgame instead of me. My face got so hot. Even after all these years, she just thinks I'm a baby.	I don't need help. I should be able to do everything on my own. My sister thinks I'm a mess. She shouldn't clean up without asking me. Katlyn thinks I'm a slob. I'm a slob. My house is a mess. I can't take care of myself. Katlyn thinks I can't take care of myself. Katlyn is nosy. Katlyn thinks I'm a child. I can't take care of my kids. Katlyn thinks I can't take care of my kids. I'm a baby. I'm not capable. Katlyn is insensitive. Katlyn doesn't trust me / believe in me. Katlyn is overbearing.

When she finished telling her story, I read my list back to her. She let me know which thoughts felt true and which ones were irrelevant. I wanted to work on the most powerful of these so we could have the greatest impact during our session. The most disturbing beliefs are the ones that, when toppled, can shake up our perspective the most.

Chana: Which thought feels the most true and the most painful at the same time?

Jane: Katlyn thinks I'm a slob.

We processed Jane's belief about her sister using *The Work* of Byron Katie. *The Work* is made up of four questions:

1. Is it true?

2. Can you absolutely know that it's true?

3. How do you react when you believe the thought?

4. Who/How would you be without the thought?

We are then asked to identify as many turnarounds (opposites) of the thought as we can and offer at least three reasons why the new thought is as true or more true than the original one. In this Inquiry, you'll see how I use *The Work* as a tool for facilitation.

Chana: Is it true that Katlyn thinks you're a slob?

Jane: Yeah.

Chana: Can you absolutely know that it's true?

Jane: Hmm... I guess I can't know for sure.

Chana: And how do you react when you believe that Katlyn thinks you're a slob?

Jane: I want to disappear. And at the same time, I want to yell at her.

Chana: Anything else?

Jane: My body gets hot and tense. I can't enjoy my sister; I just want to avoid her when she comes over.

Chana: Now, take a deep breath and imagine yourself at home with your sister. She's doing your dishes and the thought that Katlyn thinks you're a slob *isn't there.* How would you be without the thought?

Jane: Oh. That's funny. I'd be relieved. I didn't know how I was going to get through the dishes that day. My kitchen was all cleaned up by the time she was done, and it was so much easier for me to make dinner. Gosh. I don't think I even said, "Thank you."

Chana: Anything else?

Jane: Yes. I'd be more relaxed. Calmer. More open to talking and connecting to her.

Chana: So let's turn it around. What's the opposite of "Katlyn thinks you're a slob?"

Jane: Katlyn doesn't think I'm a slob.

Chana: Give me three reasons it's as true or truer than your original belief.

Jane: She never said so. She had a smile on her face while she did the dishes.

Chana: One more.

Jane: Ha. I just thought of something… When her kids were little, her house was pretty messy. Maybe she simply thinks I'm a mom with young kids and that that's a messy situation.

During our session, Jane explored more turnarounds:

I think I'm a slob.

Katlyn thinks I'm neat.

Katlyn thinks I'm a slob and that's okay.

Jane walked out of our session feeling more settled. Seeing all the beliefs from her **Rant** on paper helped her to see them with fresh eyes. She understood why she was upset and was able to continue to question her assumptions about herself and her sister until she could feel compassion and ease.

Use **The Rant** when you want to get your thoughts out in a way that's normal and comfortable, the way you'd share with a friend. You don't have to put on the "Inquiry cap" while you tell your story – you can do that later. Remember, though, that the goal of storytelling is to pull out thoughts for Inquiry – it's not just a coffee chat between friends. Once you choose a thought to work on, stay focused on Inquiry and don't sink back into the narrative. Then, use the collection of thoughts you've gleaned as your guide until you feel the issue is resolved.

Download a **Rant** worksheet from the **Free Bonus Section** of my website:

Hold.ChanaMason.com/bonus

The Survey

A compilation of commonly held limiting
beliefs that quickly reveal challenges
facing clients.

What a liberation to realize that the
"voice in my head" is not who I am.
Who am I then? The one who sees that.

nother fabulous tool for identifying thoughts is **The Survey**, which
I love using with new clients. It's also my absolute favorite tool when
doing sessions with groups. Rather than finding unique thoughts within
yourself, the **Survey** does the opposite. It uses a set of universal beliefs that
many of us have to one degree or another.

Before discussing it any further, let me show you how it works by trying
it yourself.

Let's pretend you're a new client of mine. Please complete the exercise
below before we continue. It'll only take a couple of minutes. Have fun!

Below is a list of thoughts that linger in many people's minds. Rate your level
of belief in each statement from 1 = Don't Identify to 10 = Strongly Identify.
Don't think too hard on your response; simply write a number that relates to
your first gut reaction.

1. Change is hard . . . . _____
2. I can't trust people . . . . _____
3. I should work harder . . . . _____
4. I'm not lovable . . . . _____
5. I'm not safe . . . . _____
6. If people got to know me, they wouldn't like me . . . . _____
7. There's something wrong with me . . . . _____
8. Life isn't fair . . . . _____
9. I'm not talented enough . . . . _____
10. I'm a fraud . . . . _____
11. If only I had the right look, I'd be happy . . . . _____

12.	I have to take care of everyone else........................ _____
13.	It's not realistic to go after my dreams.................... _____
14.	I can't trust myself.. _____
15.	I have to earn happiness................................... _____
16.	I'm lazy... _____
17.	I'm not experienced enough to get what I want.............. _____
18.	It matters what people think of me......................... _____
19.	My parents didn't/don't love me............................ _____
20.	I'm trapped... _____
21.	No one understands me...................................... _____
22.	I don't follow through on what I start..................... _____
23.	I'm not good enough.. _____
24.	I don't deserve to be happy................................ _____
25.	Trusting people is hard.................................... _____
26.	I need to know how things are going to turn out before I start _____
27.	Happy people are faking it................................. _____
28.	I can't sell myself.. _____
29.	Happy people are shallow................................... _____
30.	Life is hard.. _____

How'd it go? Did you find beliefs you didn't realize have been lurking in your closet?

The above **Survey** is a condensed version of one I've used in workshops and sessions as an assessment tool. It's modeled after a wealth and success **Survey** written by T. Harv Eker for his *Millionaire Mind* seminar. I attended the workshop with my husband and pre-teen son, and after we all filled it out, my son asked if we could compare notes. We laughed every time one of us scored high on a belief such as, "wealthy people are dishonest," which deflated all the fear and tension around it. My son consciously observed his parents' limiting beliefs around money and what might be holding us back from receiving abundance. It gave him an opportunity to assess the validity of these beliefs before they could become deeply ingrained in his subconscious as an adult. This experience is just one of the many reasons I love the **Survey**.

Benefits of the **Survey** process:

1. **Most people believe their thoughts are unique to them or are ashamed of them**. Having thoughts printed on paper

makes it clear they're common. We can easily talk about them without wanting to hide in a corner.

2. **It may take weeks or months to uncover many of your subconscious beliefs without a survey**. Starting with one gives you a solid foundation for discovering the beliefs that resonate most and can save time in getting to the bottom of your conflicts.

3. **You can create surveys around specific topics to uncover patterns of belief.** For example, a dating coach and I developed a survey of beliefs related to dating and relationships. We're quickly ready to see what's blocking them. By bringing these patterns up to the surface in tandem, we're able to tackle the most significant obstacles facing our clients from the get-go. You can access topic-specific surveys I've created at: Hold.ChanaMason.com/bonus

4. **They're easy to use.** Within five minutes, you can dismiss any thoughts you find ridiculous or give a 10 to those you believe to be *absolutely true*.

5. **You can use them as a reference point to measure progress.** I have my clients retake the survey every couple of sessions. We can tangibly see how much they've shifted in their beliefs and where there's still work to do. I suggest you do this as well.

I offered a health **Survey** to a client of mine; we'll call her Wendy. She came to me because she wanted to lose weight and feared her obesity was going to lead to the heart disease experienced by her parents. The **Survey** included the statement, "skinny people are shallow," which Wendy identified with the most. I suggested we focus the rest of our session inquiring about that one belief.

Chana: Is it true that skinny people are shallow?

Wendy: Yes. It feels that way.

Chana: Can you absolutely know it's true?

Wendy: Hmm. Not for sure. No.

Chana: And how do you react when you believe that skinny people are shallow?

Wendy: I feel bitter and resentful when I see thin people. Even if I don't know them, and I just see them walking down the street.

Chana: What else?

Wendy: I feel like sinking into my chair. I don't really want to do anything. It feels heavy. Actually… it makes me feel fatter.

Chana: What are you unable to do when you believe that skinny people are shallow?

Wendy: I can't think straight. I can't make good decisions. I for sure can't eat healthy stuff.

Chana: How do you benefit from believing the thought?

Wendy: The last thing I ever want to be is shallow. Like those ditsy girls in high school who were obsessed with their hair and make-up.

The upcoming question - and many throughout this book - follow the style of Barry Neil Kaufman's *Option Process*, in which we question assumptions, seek to clarify the meaning of language, and explore the necessity of our emotions. The aim is to find answers within ourselves. Some *Option* questions are:

What do you mean when you say….?

Do you need to feel angry in order to make sure you don't engage in that behavior?

Do you believe that?

How come?

Why did you do that?

How do you feel about that?

Here, I wish to lay out Wendy's logic in a simple sentence so she can assess whether it serves her.

Chana: Do you have to believe this thought that makes you feel heavy and fat in order to be a deep person?

Wendy: Oh. I never thought of it that way. I guess not. I could just keep reading and thinking and feeling…

Chana: Can you reach your weight and health goals believing that skinny people are shallow?

Wendy: Well, I want to eat healthier, but I also don't want to be shallow. Being a deep feeling and thinking person is really important to me.

Chana: So you've put yourself in a **Double Bind**. That's a situation in which you want two things that you've made mutually exclusive. You want to be lean and healthy, and you want to be a deep person, but your belief only allows for one of those.

Wendy: And being shallow seems so horrific to me that I chose to be fat.

Chana: Exactly.

Wendy: So how can I change that?

Chana: You can explore other ways of thinking, particularly those that oppose the thought you're currently believing.

Wendy: I can do that.

Chana: What's the opposite of skinny people are shallow?

Wendy: Skinny people *aren't* shallow?

Chana: Yes. Can you give me three reasons why that's true?

Wendy: No. Not really.

Chana: Do you know anyone who is skinny and deep?

Wendy: Yes. Yes, I do. There's Gene and Pamela and … Wow.

Chana: Why did you say, "Wow?"

Wendy: I just realized it's a lot of people. As soon as I thought about it, I realized how many skinny, deep people I know.

Chana: Each one of those people is a reason why it's true that skinny people aren't shallow.

Wendy: That's a lot of reasons.

Chana: Yes. Can you give me another turnaround for skinny people are shallow?

Wendy: *Fat* people are shallow.

Chana: Why is that true?

Wendy: Well, I can speak for myself. I end up spending so much time worrying how I look in my clothes when it gets really tight, and I probably shop for clothing more than my skinny friends who stay in the same dress size all the time.

Chana: And one more reason?

Wendy: There are plenty of fat folks reading *People* magazine and grooming themselves all the time.

Chana: Good to realize. Let's do one more turnaround. Perhaps make yourself the subject this time. I'm…

Wendy: I'm shallow. Ooh. That hurts. And I can see how that's true. I'm constantly looking at how others look or wondering what they think of me. I spend more time thinking about food, and I have less energy to do things because my body weighs me down.

Chana: Any other reasons?

Wendy: This is embarrassing. I assume skinny people have no depth just because of how much they weigh - can it get any more shallow than that?

Chana: You've put two human qualities, weight and depth, and correlated them. The bigger question here is whether they necessarily have anything to do with one another. Does physical size have anything to do with depth of thinking or feeling?

Wendy: You mean, does being skinny or fat have anything to do with whether you're deep or shallow?

Chana: Exactly.

Wendy: Not when I stop to think about it. You can be skinny and either deep or shallow. You could also be fat and either deep or shallow. It depends more on your personality than on your frame.

Chana: So which of these qualities do you want for yourself?

Wendy: I'd like to be thin *and* deep. That way I can be healthy, have energy, and be able to contribute more in the world.

Chana: Sounds like an inspiring goal.

Through filling out a health **Survey,** Wendy discovered some challenging beliefs she had lurking under the surface. Wendy had trapped herself in a bind by believing that she'd be missing out on one of her core values, depth, if she worked on one of her life goals, losing weight. By engaging in Inquiry, she was able to see how much suffering she was causing herself with this belief, but also how untrue it was when she faced it head-on.

Use **The Survey** when you want to quickly get to the core of what you are facing. You'll easily gather beliefs for Inquiry. Surveys are versatile, can be as long as you want, and can focus on a topic relevant to you or your specific client population. They're great for working with groups since they illustrate that many of us are struggling with the same beliefs.

Download sample **Surveys** in the **Free Bonus section** of my website:

Hold.ChanaMason.com/bonus.

The Thought Bank

A collection of thoughts or beliefs that
cause a person distress.

People who have no hold over their process of thinking are likely to be ruined by liberty of thought. If thought is immature, liberty of thought becomes a method of converting men into animals.

- Muhammad Iqbal

C indy came to me because she was feeling unhappy and unfulfilled with her life.

Chana: What's upsetting you?

Cindy: I'm really frustrated with homemaking.

Chana: What about homemaking frustrates you?

Cindy: Well, I want my house to be well kept, but I resent all the work involved.

Chana: What about the work do you resent?

Cindy: I don't know… Just everything! Everything about keeping my house together annoys me these days.

Because of Cindy's lack of specificity, I decide it would be best to give her cues, the first words of a belief for her to complete. Cues can help clarify what we really believe. To get everything out on paper quickly, I suggest we build a **Thought Bank** on the topic of homemaking. I ask Cindy to complete the following sentences:

Cleaning is _____

Cleaning should be _____

In regards to housekeeping, I should _____

Cooking is _____

Cooking should be _____

In regards to cooking, I should _____

I shouldn't have to _____

Being a homemaker means _____

As a homemaker, I should _____

Cindy was able to focus on completing the sentences and was no longer distracted by the mess in her head about the mess in her house. Here are some of her beliefs:

Cleaning is a chore.

Cleaning should be easy.

I shouldn't have to pick up after everyone.

Cooking should be fun.

Cooking is overwhelming.

Being a homemaker means putting everyone else first.

As a homemaker, I should always have a smile on my face.

In about fifteen minutes, Cindy and I have built a **Thought Bank** we can use for numerous sessions.

Chana: (after rereading the list to Cindy) Now do you understand why you're so resentful?

Cindy: Oh yeah! It's kind of hard not to be frustrated when this is what I have inside.

Chana: Exactly. Now let's take another look at your list. Which thought feels the truest and at the same time the most upsetting?

Cindy: *Being a homemaker means putting everyone else first.*

Chana: Being a homemaker means putting everyone else first. Is it true?

Cindy: Yes.

Chana: Can you absolutely know that it's true?

Cindy: It sure feels like it, yes.

Chana: And how do you react when you believe that being a homemaker means putting everyone else first?

Cindy: I feel rebellious. I want to fight everyone and everything.

Chana: Anything else?

Cindy: I get tired. And really lazy.

Chana: What are you afraid would happen if you didn't believe the thought?

Cindy: That I wouldn't get anything done. That I'd just sit and watch garbage on TV all day.

Chana: Does believing the thought motivate you to get stuff done?

Cindy: Oh….

Chana: Why did you just say that?

Cindy: I just realized it's exactly the opposite of what I was hoping. Believing I have to put everyone else first feels like so much pressure that I hide behind my favorite magazine and put off doing the laundry.

Chana: Take a deep breath and image yourself in front of the laundry pile without the thought that being a homemaker means putting everyone else first. How would you be without it?

Cindy: Calmer. The laundry feels less scary, actually.

Chana: What's the opposite of being a homemaker means putting everyone else first?

Cindy: Being a homemaker doesn't mean putting everyone else first.

Chana: How is that true?

Cindy: When I'm sick, the whole house falls apart, so I need to take care of myself.

Chana: What else?

Cindy: If I do *everything* myself, I don't give my kids the opportunity to help out.

Chana: What's a third reason?

Cindy: If I don't do this in a balanced way, I'll be grumpy all the time. I think my kids would rather have a messy house than a grouchy mom. So would my husband, that's for sure.

Cindy and I explored other turnarounds until she came to see that taking care of herself was the best way she could keep her home a place everyone, including herself, wanted to be. At the beginning of each of our next sessions together, I reread the list to Cindy, and we crossed out the limiting beliefs that no longer resonated. Sometimes we found new beliefs to add to her **Thought Bank** and wrote those down. Over time, the list dwindled to nothing and we knew our work in this area was done. One desperate housewife, slightly less desperate!

Like your local branch of Citizens Bank has a stockpile of cash to withdraw, your head holds mounds of thoughts about everything. When they're stuck in your mind, it's as if they're locked in the vault. Getting thoughts out on paper is like putting them on the teller's counter, clearly spread out before you.

A decade ago, a group of my female friends, all moms, got together every week to engage and build skills in Inquiry. Sometimes we focused our energy on facilitating one woman through a specific challenge she was facing in her life. Other times, we wanted to focus on an area affecting all of us, such as motherhood. We started by building a **Thought Bank** of beliefs we could work on for a few weeks. In one particular meeting, each of us wrote at the top of our page:

Mothers should _____

To this, we collectively responded:

Mothers should help kids with homework.

Mothers should be warm.

Mothers should cook healthy meals.

Mothers should smile all the time.

Mothers should enjoy nursing.

Mothers should be patient.

Mothers should love their kids all the time.

Mothers should enjoy playing games.

We quickly gleaned a whole collection of beliefs we could use as fuel for Inquiry. At times, one of us would write something the others hadn't thought to include, but the minute she said it, we all laughed (or cried) in agreement. Some thoughts made some women stressed, but brought me and others tremendous joy, such as, *Mothers should cook healthy meals.* I happen to love health, nutrition, and cooking, so it's a pleasure for me to live that way. For others, the kitchen is a boring or frustrating place, so they felt tremendous frustration when they believed that thought.

One woman, Meredith, was particularly triggered by the thought, "Mothers should enjoy playing games." We facilitated the Inquiry process with her as a group, which meant that we took turns asking questions or sharing feedback. For the sake of simplicity, I'm gathering all of our voices into one: "Group."

Meredith: I can't stand games.

Group: So why do you think you should like them?

Meredith: I don't know. It's what kids like.

Group: Did you like them when you were a kid?

Meredith: (laughs) No, actually. I've never liked them.

Group: So why do you assume that it's what kids like?

Meredith: I guess I always thought I was weird. My family all liked playing games - everyone but me.

Group: So was it helpful for you growing up to have a mother who believed that, "Mothers should enjoy playing games?"

Meredith: No. She kept wanting to play with me. It felt like so much pressure. I think she believed kids should enjoy playing games, but that wasn't me.

Group: How do you react when you believe it *should* be you?

Meredith: I get stiff. My neck gets tight.

Group: Anything else?

Meredith: Yeah, it's like I've been punched in the stomach.

Group: Whose business are you in when you believe you should enjoy playing games? (Your **Business** is that over which you have total control and power to change. We'll delve deep into this concept in the chapter **There's No Business Like Your Business.**)

Meredith: It feels like I'm in my business, but really, it's more like I'm in my kids' business - like their lives will be ruined if I don't play with them. I can't know for sure that playing games is what they need from me.

Group: Why don't you try turning it around? What's the opposite of you should enjoy playing games?

Meredith: I shouldn't enjoy playing games.

Group: Why?

Meredith: Well, because I don't.

Group: Two more reasons...

Meredith: Because I read to them a lot and maybe if we played together, that wouldn't happen as much.

Group: Why else?

Meredith: I'm stuck. Does anyone have an idea?

Group: I do. I've been trying to teach my preteen to seek outside help when he needs something. I just don't have time to help him with all his projects. So for me, another reason not to do something your kids like is so they can learn to get their needs met in other ways. I don't know if it's healthy to have one person being the address for everything.

Meredith: I never thought of that. I like it.

Group: I have another one. I hate it when my mom is fake with me and pretends to take an interest in something she finds dull. I'd rather she say she's not interested and we can connect on something we both like.

Meredith: So it's okay for me not to like playing games?

Group: Is it the truth?

Meredith: Yeah.

Group: That's the mom your kids got.

Meredith: It still somehow feels like not enough.

Group: What's not enough?

Meredith: They want to play games and I won't. I can tell it makes them sad.

Group: The bigger question is one of creativity. Are you the only way they can get this need met?

Meredith: Who would play games with my kids?

Group: I have an idea. You read to your kids but won't play games. I hate reading out loud. How about you send your kids to my house for games and you can read to mine?

Meredith: Deal!

The **Thought Bank** brought my women's group closer together. We saw how much commonality we shared, and we felt less isolated. We did Inquiry on many of the beliefs as a collective, which made the process feel light and playful, and since the **Thought Bank** was on paper, we could go back to it as a reference any time.

Note: The purpose of a **Thought Bank** is to collect beliefs for Inquiry. It's crucial when exploring a belief that it be rooted in a specific situation. *Mothers should be warm* is best inquired when I'm visualizing the day I was in the kitchen, exhausted and cleaning up the burnt rice when my kid walked in the door from school. Specificity allows me to pin down not only my collection of beliefs around an event but also a tangible set of reactions to those beliefs.

Use **The Thought Bank** when you want to flesh out all your beliefs about a topic. **The Rant** weaves in nicely with **The Thought Bank .** It's also a fantastic tool when facilitating groups in therapy or workshops. The process unites the members of the group and helps them dissipate any identification with or shame around the thoughts they believe.

Download a **Thought Bank** worksheet from
the **Free Bonus Section** of my website:
Hold.ChanaMason.com/bonus.

The ATM

Asking **And That Means** accesses
the limiting beliefs underlying
the words you are expressing.

In the space between stimulus (what happens) and how we respond, lies our freedom to choose. Ultimately, this power to choose is what defines us as human beings. We may have limited choices but we can always choose. We can choose our thoughts, emotions, moods, our words, our actions; we can choose our values and live by principles. It is the choice of acting or being acted upon.

- Stephen Covey

Eileen suffered from frequent panic attacks and constant low-grade anxiety. These feelings were overwhelming and blocked her ability to think straight and live with purpose. We had the following session the day after a particularly intense attack.

Eileen: I've been hunting for an apartment, and it's so stressful.

Chana: Why is it stressful for you?

Eileen: Because sometimes the landlord will sign with someone else before I've even gotten to see a place. Or I find a great place with three bedrooms, but I only have one roommate so far.

Chana: And why is that stressful?

Eileen: Because I don't know what's going to happen.

Chana: And why is that challenging?

Eileen: Because I'm totally not in control!

So far we're able to glean a few of Eileen's beliefs:

She needs to know what's going to happen.

She's not in control.

She needs to have her roommate situation totally figured out before she signs anything.

Looking at apartments might be a waste of time.

It's easiest to focus on one thought at a time, so let's ask Eileen to choose the one with which she most identifies:

Eileen: For sure the fact that I'm not in control.

Chana: You're not in control. Is it true?

Eileen: Yes! Totally!

Chana: Can you absolutely know that it's true that you're not in control?

Eileen: Yes.

Chana: How do you react when you believe the thought that you're not in control?

Eileen: My chest tightens. It's hard to breathe. My vision starts to fog up.

Chana: What else?

Eileen: I want to put my hands over my head and hide under my bed. It's like the whole world is coming crashing down.

Chana: Take a deep breath. Good. Now imagine yourself in that same situation, but the thought that you're not in control isn't there. Who are you without it?

Eileen: I'm just me, I guess. My body has chilled out. I'm just standing in the apartment I'm checking out and enjoying how much light it has. I'm excited about living there.

Chana: What is the opposite of "you're not in control?"

Eileen: I am in control.

Chana: Give me three reasons why that's true.

Eileen: I can decide what I chose to focus on in the situation. I can decide who I talk to and which apartments I visit.

Chana: Great. What else?

Eileen: I decide how I react to the landlords.

Chana: Can you think of another turnaround?

One of the ways we can turn a statement around is by replacing the subject with "my thinking." Our thinking brings thoughts to our attention without my conscious control. Ideally, we want our beliefs to serve us, not enslave us, so putting the seat of our thoughts in its place can help us take back the reigns.

Eileen: My thinking is not in control.

Chana: Fantastic. Can you think of three reasons why that's as true or truer than your original thought?

Eileen: Well, my thinking can't actually *do* anything. It just comes up with all these potential situations or failures or problems. But I'm the one who shows up or signs the contract or finds the roommates.

Chana: Yes. And can you think of one more turnaround?

Eileen: Um…. I don't think so…

Chana: How about, I'm not in control and –

Eileen: And that's *okay?*

Chana: Yes.

Eileen: No. No way. That is so not okay!

The reality is we're not in control of most of what happens in life. Eileen has no control over landlords, roommates, apartment availability, or even a roach infestation. It's true that she can control her *reactions* to these things, but what's upsetting Eileen the most is that she can't control the circumstances themselves. There's something deeper going on, something lurking under the surface.

To help Eileen get a better grasp of the beliefs she has stored under the surface, we need to pull another tool out of the drawer. Let's step up to her cerebral **Thought Bank** and use the **ATM,** which stands for **And That Means**:

Chana: Perhaps the idea that you're not in control is not really what upsets you. Let's dig a bit deeper. I'd like you to complete the following sentence in as many ways as feels true for you. You don't have control, ***And That Means***:

Eileen: That means that…
>　　　 … *I'm in danger*
>　　　 … *things won't work out how I want.*
>　　　 … *it's the worst case scenario.*

... my anxiety won't get better.
... I won't make it financially.
... I won't find the right guy.
... I won't be able to make it.

I read this list back to Eileen and asked her to identify the statement which caused her the most upset and felt simultaneously the truest.

Eileen: I'm in danger.

Chana: You're not in control and that means you're in danger, is it true?

Eileen: (Crying) Yes.

Chana: Why are you crying?

Eileen: Because I'm so scared.

Chana: Why are you scared?

Eileen: I guess because I know that I'm not in control. That everything is totally out of control. And no one can protect me from all of the craziness out there.

Chana: So if you're not in control, that means that everything is totally out of control?

Eileen: Yes.

Chana: Everything is totally out of control, is it true?

Eileen: Yes.

Chana: Can you absolutely know that it's true?

Eileen: Hmm.

Chana: Why did you say, "Hmm?"

Eileen: There are so many things in the world, like birds and trees and the wind and other people and what they do. They're not in my control, but there seems to be some sort of order to them. I can't say for sure that it's all out of control.

Chana: And how do you react when you believe that it is out of control?

Eileen: My whole body tightens. I want to curl up in a ball and hide under the covers. It's like the entire world is going to collapse and every bad guy is going to get me.

Chana: What are you unable to do when you believe everything is out of control?

Eileen: I'm too tight and scared to do anything fun. I can't think straight. It's so depressing!

Chana: Here's a more challenging question: how do you benefit from believing that everything is out of control?

Eileen: It's my job to control everything. I get to be the pilot, the commander in chief. It feels really powerful, like… oh.

Chana: Like what?

Eileen: Like I'm G-d. (Laughs.)

Chana: Why did you laugh?

Eileen: I'm so *not* G-d. But I think my ego loves the idea of me being in charge.

Chana: Let's take a step back. Take a deep breath and imagine yourself back in the apartment search, only this time without the thought that everything is out of control. How are you without the thought?

Eileen: I feel more relaxed. There's a part of me that knows everything's going to work out somehow - even though I don't know the details of how.

Chana: Feel that. This is the calm you've been looking for.

Eileen: Yeah.

Chana: And you can have it even without knowing what is coming next.

Eileen: Right.

Chana: So let's turn it around. What's the opposite of everything is out of control?

Eileen: Everything is in control.

Chana: How is that true?

Eileen: Well, back to the birds and the trees, they keep doing what they do and flying and growing in a way that seems orderly.

Chana: What else?

Eileen: There's a system for looking for apartments. People post places with phone numbers, and I can go and see them. It makes sense mostly. It's not like I get there and the tenants think I'm a door-to-door saleswoman or something. When they post a price, I can trust that it's really the price. Landlords are honest most of the time, actually.

Chana: Can you give me one more reason why everything is in control?

Eileen: If I walk down the street I see people mostly following rules and being nice to each other.

Chana: How about another turnaround?

Eileen: Everything is not out of control?

Chana: Yes. How is that true?

Eileen: Well... stores open and close at fixed times, machines usually work the way they're supposed to. And there are those videos of thousands of cars all going where they need to go, and it all seems like a dance.

Chana: You came up with that pretty fast.

Eileen: I did.

Chana: How?

Eileen: I don't know. When you asked the question, I suddenly saw all these images in my head of stuff I usually don't pay attention to.

Chana: You asked your mind for information, and it gave it to you.

Eileen: Yes.

Chana: That sounds like a pretty reliable system.

Eileen: Whoa!

Chana: Why did you just say that?

Eileen: I tend to focus on scary things like the world being out of control, and when I do that I see images of terrorist attacks and car accidents and mobs. It's like I press a button and my mind spits out results.

Chana: What do you want to do?

Eileen: Press better buttons. I want to focus on how the world is in control and trust that I'm safe and okay.

Chana: How can you do that?

Eileen: Hmm… I guess when I'm walking down the street, and I see cars stopping at a red light and all the passengers being safe, I can remind myself that it's an example of the world being in control. I can do that with lots of things.

Chana: How do you feel?

Eileen: Better. I don't know how, but in my gut, I *know* the apartment is going to work out. And in the meantime, I'm okay. Even this conversation has been pretty "in control."

With Eileen's concerns out in the open, we were able to work on the beliefs at the root of her anxiety. Over time, she was able to shift her subconscious experience of the world being a scary and unreliable place to one that aligned with her intellectual and religious beliefs about living in a loving universe.

As we saw with Eileen, the source of our upset is never facts of life such as:

It's raining outside.

I'm forty years old.

My cat died.

Sharon says she doesn't like me.

My pants are tight at the waist.

Our distress comes from the *meaning* we attribute to these facts – that's what you want to inquire about. The easiest way to access that meaning to walk right up to the **ATM** and pop in your question. So, for example, Marty came to me for dating advice complaining that his weight would mean he could never get married. In particular, he was embarrassed about his tight pants.

Chana: Your pants are tight at the waist, **And That Means**…

Marty: … *I'm too fat.*

… *women won't find me attractive.*

… *I should lose weight.*

… *I'm disgusting.*

… *I should give up on dating.*

When Marty believed the above thoughts, he couldn't help but suffer. Doing Inquiry on them brought him back to a calm and open place, one from which he could more readily accept himself and have the courage to date.

What drives our emotions and behavior is the *meaning* that we apply to stimuli. Below is a list of observations that don't intrinsically have any significance. By asking **And That Means**, we can tap into the story we've built around the stimulus.

Stimulus: Ally got into a car accident.

ATM: Ally is unlucky.

Stimulus: It's raining on my wedding day.

ATM: My wedding is ruined.

Stimulus: Grandma died.

ATM: I'll never be loved that way again.

Stimulus: We had pizza for dinner.

ATM: I should go on a diet.

Clients are sometimes confused by the difference between facts and beliefs. Ally, for example, might believe her lack of luck is a "fact of life," which makes it difficult for her to question its validity. It can be helpful to ask, "Would every human on earth come to the same conclusion about that event?" Ally can realize that others might conclude:

Ally's very lucky to be alive.

Seat belts are important.

We need to create stronger legislation around road rage.

It's better to walk than to drive.

Each of these beliefs would lead to an entirely different outlook on life, feelings, and behaviors; in other words, a different life altogether. Ally can then question whether believing she's unlucky is her only option and whether it's leading her to the happy, peaceful state she's hoping to experience.

Often, we might believe our frustration, anger, or sadness exist for no reason, but there's always a method to our madness. Taking a moment to understand what meaning we've assigned to a given stimulus gives us the opportunity to choose kinder ways of thinking and being.

Use **The ATM** when your agitation seems disproportionate to the situation or when you don't seem to be shifting after doing Inquiry on the thoughts at hand. **And That Means** will help you withdraw a whole collection of baggage from your mind's vault, and unlike a Citizens Bank ATM, you won't get charged any fees!

Tower of Babble

A web of beliefs that together support
a strong uber-belief.

Every thought you produce, anything you say, any action you do, it bears your signature.

- Thich Nhat Hanh

Just like the biblical Tower of Babel, which was designed to reach to the sky and challenge the heavens, we build fortified structures of negative thoughts that hold a greater belief together. These **Towers of Babble** are always doomed to fail, but the higher they get, the harder they are to knock down. Doing Inquiry on the big belief won't be enough; we have to knock down the pillars of thought holding it up. Andrew trapped himself atop of such a **Tower of Babble**:

Andrew: I feel stuck in my life.

Chana: Why do you feel stuck?

Andrew: I really hate my job. It just sucks.

Chana: When you're in a situation you dislike, you can either change your perception, change the situation itself, or exit. Which of those most speaks to you?

Andrew: I'd really like to leave. I don't want to be in accounting. The people at work are nice, my boss is great, but accounting is soooo boring. I just want out.

Chana: Have you considered what you'd do if you did exit?

Andrew: I kind of want to start my own business selling hockey equipment.

Chana: So are you going to do that?

Andrew: I don't know. It's just too hard.

Chana: What about it is so hard?

Andrew: I've never started a business before.

Chana: So you're afraid you don't have enough experience?

Andrew: Yeah. But not just that. I mean, I'm not so charming. I don't think people would buy from me.

Chana: Anything else holding you back?

Andrew: Yeah, I mean, the business climate is not what it used to be.

Chana: What else?

Andrew: Look at me, I'm not exactly a strapping lad like Bill Gates or Zuckerberg were. I'm too old to start something new.

Chana: So you're too old, too inexperienced, and not charming. Is that it?

Andrew: Also, I'd need financial backing from family to make it. My parents are dirt poor.

Chana: And -

Andrew: And it's so much work to start a business. I don't think I have that kind of stamina.

Chana: What if you were able to muster the stamina to make it happen?

Andrew: Then what if I fail? I mean, most businesses do. Could I actually handle the possibility of that?

Chana: Anything else holding you back?

Andrew: I don't think so. I think we've pretty much nailed all my concerns.

Chana: No wonder you feel stuck. You've built a sturdy **Tower of Babble**!

As with a real building, it's easier to knock down the central pillars in the **Tower of Babble** than to try to topple the whole structure all at once. In Andrew's case, a collection of pillars held up the belief that he couldn't go out on his own and open a hockey supply business:

It's too hard.

Since I've never opened up my own business, I'm likely to fail.

I don't have enough experience.

I'm too old.

I need financial backing from family to succeed.

I'm not charming enough.

I don't have enough stamina.

The business climate is not what it needs to be.

I couldn't handle failing at business.

That's NINE beliefs! Andrew constructed such a solid foundation of limiting beliefs that he needed to knock down several pillars before the tower could topple, and that's what we did. We delved into Inquiry on the most potent of the above beliefs. After shifting five of them, the rest started to feel humorous rather than threatening. Without any divine intervention, Andrew's **Tower of Babble** went tumbling down!

Identify the key thoughts holding up a **Tower of Babble** when you are overwhelmed by a particularly challenging belief. Uncovering all the thought pillars holding up your feelings of unworthiness or incapacitation can help you face your fears and move forward.

Just Desserts Chart

A tool that helps us clarify all the reasons we feel we deserve the junk we've got and don't deserve the cake we want.

All that we are is the result
of what we have thought.

—Buddha

Melanie kept dating the "wrong kind of guy" over and over again and wanted to change her pattern. She dreamed of building a family with a caring, supportive, and communicative man with whom she could connect deeply, but she feared that if she didn't break her pattern, she'd be stuck dating "losers" for the rest of her life.

I asked Melanie to visualize her life ten years into the future with a man that she considered a "winner." She was able to see everything from what their home would look like to how they'd spend their time together. We wrote the whole vision down in detail, and I had her visualize it repeatedly as homework.

Melanie complained about having a difficult time doing the visualization at home. "It just doesn't feel believable." She found getting a crystal clear image challenging. As a way of building a solid **Thought Bank** on this topic, I gave her the homework assignment of completing what I call a **Just Desserts Chart**. Such a chart collects all the beliefs supporting the **Tower of Babble** on why Melanie wasn't moving forward in this area of her life. Melanie had beliefs holding her back and others blocking her from moving forward. These beliefs brought about her "**Just Desserts**" - what she believed she deserved in life. She was getting a cheap fast-food milkshake rather than the luxurious chocolate-fondue she wanted merely because her belief system didn't allow her to ask for or receive anything better.

I asked Melanie to list the reasons that supported the statements at the top of the chart. You can see some of her responses below:

Why I deserve to date the "losers."	Why I don't deserve a "winner."
It's all I've ever known.	Guys like that don't exist.
Guys like that are easy to meet.	There's probably not someone out there for me.
I'm more comfortable around them.	A good guy wouldn't be interested in me.
They like me.	I would probably take advantage of a good guy.
I can take care of them.	I'm not worthy of someone that good.
They make me feel special.	Wanting someone like that would set me up for disappointment.

Using the **Just Desserts Chart**, Melanie was able to build a **Thought Bank** that served as the basis for the next few sessions. We did Inquiry on most of the list until Melanie could enjoy visualizing her dream relationship and align her behavior towards manifesting it.

Bringing up the subconscious thoughts that drive our behavior makes personal growth work more effective, especially when we get the decadent dessert we desire as a reward.

Use a **Just Desserts Chart** when you want change but are deeply attached to or comfortable in your present situation.

Download a **Just Desserts** worksheet from the
Free Bonus Section of my website:
Hold.ChanaMason.com/bonus.

The Obstacle Course

A technique for visualizing the
limiting beliefs that are standing
between you and your dreams.

Surely there is grandeur in knowing that in the realm of thought, at least, you are without a chain; that you have the right to explore all heights and depth; that there are no walls nor fences, nor prohibited places, nor sacred corners in all the vast expanse of thought.

—Robert Green Ingersoll

I love helping a client develop an inspiring and exciting vision for their future and build a plan for actualizing it. I'm deeply aware, though, that if their blueprint of themselves, life, and reality is not in alignment with that vision, they'll most likely fail to follow through on their plan, or they'll find a way to sabotage it. Before working on a plan, I aim to draw out all the limiting beliefs that may hold my client back from manifesting their dream.

Dan, for instance, was plagued by thoughts that prevented him from moving his professional life forward:

Chana: What are you doing professionally now?

Dan: Well, I wouldn't call it "professional" exactly. I'm just waiting tables at a café.

Chana: Why don't you call it professional?

Dan: Cause it's just a job to pay the bills. It's not really what I want to do.

Chana: Why not?

Dan: It doesn't pay well. And the hours aren't great. But mostly, I don't like working for other people.

Chana: So you want to go into business for yourself?

Dan: Maybe.

Chana: Why the "maybe?"

Dan: It's kind of silly.

Chana: What is?

Dan: What I kind of want to do.

Chana: And what is that?

Dan: Pottery. I've been doing it as a hobby for a couple of years now. The few hours I'm in my teacher's studio are my favorite hours of the whole week.

Chana: So you want to be a potter?

Dan: My teacher says I'm quite talented. But…

Chana: But what?

Dan: Isn't it crazy?

Chana: What's crazy?

Dan: Being a potter. I couldn't really *do* that.

Chana: Hmm. What if, just for the sake of argument, it wasn't crazy? If the thought that being a potter is crazy wasn't there, could you consider the possibility?

Dan: Maybe…

Chana: Would you be willing to imagine it just for a few minutes?

Dan: I suppose I could do that.

Chana: Great. Close your eyes. (*Dan took some moments to breathe deeply and relax.*) Imagine you're five years in the future. You're working as a potter. What do you see?

Dan: I have my own studio. It's on the side of my home and faces a lake. There are huge glass windows so that natural light fills the studio most of the day.

Chana: What else do you see?

Dan: I'm making commissioned works for galleries and restaurants. I also sell pieces from my home. I'm newly married, and my wife loves eating out of the dishes I make. She really supports my work.

Chana: How are things for you financially in this vision?

Dan: We're doing just fine. We live in a rural area so our cost of living isn't so high, and we're able to grow much of our food. It's beautiful. Also, I'm constantly improving my craft, and I'm pretty good. I can support us with the pottery that I sell.

Chana: How does it feel to look at that vision?

Dan: Pretty good.

Chana: Not amazing?

Dan: Well, it's kind of fun to talk about, but hard to believe. Getting a clear image of everything is hard. It's blurry and mostly black and white.

Chana: So something is standing between you and the vision?

Dan: Yeah. Like a fog.

Limiting beliefs can block us from going after our goals. For Dan, they're presenting themselves as fog. Rather than trying to overcome something so intangible, it's easier to work with actual words. The **Obstacle Course** technique helps us gather them. We'll encourage Dan to give voice to the obstacles blocking him from moving forward by personifying his fog and having it "speak out" his fears. As you read the dialogue, I'd like to challenge you to take notes and create a **Thought Bank** of Dan's stated and implied fears.

Chana: If you could give that fog a voice, what would it say?

Dan: That pottery is totally impractical. There's no way I could ever make money doing that.

Chana: What else?

Dan: No way I could marry a woman that nice and that beautiful.

Chana: Why not?

Dan: I'm just not handsome or charming or good enough for that. Besides, I have, like, NO money.

Chana: What else does the fog say?

Dan: That I've always lived in a city and it's ridiculous to think I would ever *actually* move to a lake. I could never pull that off. It's just a pipe dream, like from a movie or something.

Chana: What else does the fog say?

Dan: That I could never get good enough at pottery to make money from it. That I could never get good enough to make pieces as stunning as I see in the vision. You have to be really special or talented or go to art school for *years* to get that good.

Chana: Anything else?

Dan: This is just a fantasy. It's out of touch with reality.

Chana: Hmm.

Dan: And that I should do something practical like get certified in accounting or get a stable job. That way I can attract a nice girl and support a family. You can't support a family with clay and glaze. Let's get real.

Dan's built himself a pretty robust **Obstacle Course**. His blueprint of beliefs about himself, the world, and what's possible blocked his ability to envision a future of his dreams. Here are some of the beliefs getting in his way:

Pottery isn't practical.

I could never attract the woman of my dreams.

It's not realistic to think I would move to the country.

I could never support a family with pottery.

I don't have enough money to attract a great woman.

I could never get good at pottery.

We did Inquiry on these thoughts and more. Every session, Dan closed his eyes and repeated the visualization. The picture got clearer until it was so believable the image was in color, and he could smell the scent of the clay and hear his wife's voice. As we neutralized his **Obstacle Course** of limiting beliefs, Dan shot down the clay pigeons blocking his path and got increasingly excited about his vision for the future and his ability to actualize it.

Use the **Obstacle Course** technique when you're feeling blocked from visualizing or actualizing your dreams. Giving voice to the hurdles getting in your way shows you were Inquiry is needed. Questioning your thinking will help you jump over those hurdles and race towards your dreams.

Download an **Obstacle Course** worksheet from the **Free Bonus Section** of my website:

Hold.ChanaMason.com/bonus.

Words to Suffer By:
DISSECTING YOUR SUFFERING

The most beautiful people we have known are those who have known defeat, known suffering, known struggle, known loss, and have found their way out of those depths.

Elisabeth Kubler-Ross

One of my spiritual teachers, Joan Laimon, says, "Consciousness creates reality." In other words, what we believe is what we get. Not only do our beliefs shape us, but the language we use also has a poignant effect on our emotions. Words are our most powerful tools for building our lives from the bottom up - word by word. Now that you've learned to identify the beliefs in your arsenal, we can dig deeper into understanding how you're affected by the words that make up those beliefs. In this section, we'll delve into all the ways language can trip us up and lead us into dark tunnels of distress. Hopefully, you will become more conscious of your word choices and use them to shape a beautiful, peaceful, and joyous world.

Should-Ing Belongs in the Outhouse

A word that argues with reality and brings
people upset, frustration, and worry.

Stop should-ing all over yourself!

- Tony Robbins

Although most of us believe **Should** is a sweet expression of preference, we actually use it to fiercely argue with reality and say that what "is" shouldn't be. Byron Katie says that when we argue with reality, we always lose because reality is what it *is*. It's not changing, and our lack of acceptance can only lead to disappointment.

When I teach a workshop and introduce the problematic nature of the word **Should**, I invariably get backlash from the audience. One person will want to push the word to its ultimate limit by bringing up the evils of violence. Living in Jerusalem, this usually comes up as terrorism. A few years ago, Jerusalem found itself in the middle of the "Stabbing Intifada," during which terrorists stabbed civilians in the streets of our city. About a dozen stabbings over the course of the year inspired reverberations of fear into the hearts of many Israelis, including my students. During a workshop, the heat in the room led to this:

Sandy: But what about the stabbings that have been going on? You can't just accept them as okay! People are getting hurt. It's scary.

Chana: So you believe that *people **shouldn't** stab other people.*

Sandy: Of course! You don't actually think they should, do you?

Chana: Rather than share with you what I think, I suggest we go deeper into understanding the word **should.**

I walked up to the board and asked the group to define the word **should**. This is what they said:

It would be better.   *There's no other way.*

It's right.   *Obligation.*

It would be ideal.   *I expect it.*

It must be.   *It has to be.*

It's correct.

Chana: Sandy, tell me, what do you see in reality? Do people stab other people sometimes?

Sandy: Yeah…

Chana: So, basically, G-d or reality or the universe or whatever you want to call it has created a world in which people stab other people. And that creation is all wrong.

Sandy: Yes. It's like a kink in the system.

Chana: So you know better.

Sandy: Yeah.

Chana: If you were running the world, people wouldn't be stabbing other people.

Sandy: For sure not.

Chana: The question is: do you rule the world?

Sandy: Of course not.

Chana: Then you are simply arguing with reality. And when you argue with reality, you will always lose the argument.

Sandy: Why?

Chana: Because reality is going to do what it's going to do. People die, earthquakes shake, and bad movies come out every summer. You can't control it all.

Sandy: So when I think that people shouldn't stab other people I'm just in a fight?

Chana: Yes! You are living in a city where stabbings are happening, but you're trying to cover your eyes and pretend they're not happening. How do you feel inside when you believe people shouldn't stab other people?

Sandy: I get intensely mad. My fists clench. My teeth clench. I want to punch somebody.

Chana: So when you believe that thought, you become violent. You inhabit the violence you believe shouldn't exist in the world.

Sandy: Oh… Yeah. I guess I do.

Chana: Perhaps, rather than trying to control other people and their knives, you could turn the thought around and see how it applies to you.

Sandy: So *I shouldn't stab other people?* But I've never hurt anyone.

Chana: Have you ever said or done something to another person that felt like a "stab in the back?"

Sandy: Um…. Oh, yeah… I ditched a friend the other night to hang out with a guy I thought was cute. It was so not cool.

Chana: So you have where to grow in this area.

Sandy: Totally. I didn't cut into her flesh, but I hurt her. I should apologize.

Chana: If you did, you'd feel more peaceful inside.

Sandy: Yeah. I feel pretty guilty about it.

Chana: Yes. Can you give more reasons why it's true that you shouldn't stab other people?

Sandy: I don't literally stab other people.

Chana: That's comforting for me to hear. Two more reasons?

Sandy: I don't want to kill anyone?

Chana: And one more?

Sandy: Um…. I can't think of anything….

Chana: Tell me, since you arrived in Jerusalem last month, how many people have been stabbed?

Sandy: I don't know for sure. Maybe twelve.

Chana: That's a pretty good guess. There have been three stabbings, actually. And tell me, how many stabbings have you replayed in your mind?

Sandy: Soooo many. Every time I walk in the Old City and see an Arab, I picture them pulling out a knife and am on the lookout. Or if I read about a stabbing in the news, I picture it over and over in my head. It freaks me out.

Chana: You don't like feeling freaked out, I presume?

Sandy: Not at all.

Chana: So it might be a good idea to stop stabbing other people.

Sandy: But I'm not…?

Chana: In your head.

Sandy: Oh. I get it. Yeah. That would be nice.

Chana: You're looking for people to stop stabbing other people so you can feel peaceful.

Sandy: Yeah.

Chana: Perhaps skip the middleman. You can feel more peaceful by not stabbing others in the back or replaying those images in your head.

Sandy: I see that.

Chana: And by not arguing with reality. People stab other people. That's the reality.

Sandy: But I don't want them to.

Chana: I hear that. Can you control what the million people in this city do?

Sandy: No.

Chana: Who can you control?

Sandy: Just me.

Chana: So start with you. Don't stab people. Not in your head and not in the physical world. Teach us about nonviolence and kindness through your example.

Sandy: I can try.

Chana: That's what we're all doing – trying.

One fascinating byproduct of **Should** statements is that they always lead us in the opposite direction from what we intended. Though Sandy believed the thought *people shouldn't stab other people* would make the world more peaceful, it actually made *her* a more angry and violent person. This is also the case with all sorts of other **Should** statements, such as *I should exercise, I should work harder, people should be polite*. But don't take my word for it, get a taste of this axiom for yourself. I'd like you to do an exercise I use with clients who struggle with obesity.

Close your eyes and imagine you are standing a few steps away from a long table. On top of that table are all of your most favorite treats and desserts. Allow yourself to get very detailed in your vision. What colors do you see? What do you smell? How do you react when you believe that *you shouldn't eat those desserts*?

If you are like most people, visualizing the desserts on the table created a desire for them and believing that *you shouldn't eat the desserts* pushed you towards scarfing down everything on display. It's an ironic result of our attempts to take care of ourselves. It's also why I believe dieting often doesn't work: ineffective levels of guilt, shame, and anger are at play. Barry Neil Kaufman points out that we make ourselves unhappy because we've been conditioned to believe that unhappiness will motivate us to engage in beneficial behaviors. The problem is that unhappiness fuels our destructive actions in the first place. We'll discuss this further in **The Addiction Loop and Aggression Tailspin**.

Sandy was fearful and angry in response to the terrorism that she experienced in her city. She came to realize her upset was due to her story about that reality:

that it was wrong, a "kink in the system," and that it **should** be different. She suffered under the barrage of images she projected in her mind and the internal violence they created. **Should-ing** all over herself left her powerless to develop peace in herself and, ultimately, the world.

Should-ing Belongs in the Outhouse because the word **Should** causes us so much internal strife (and possibly gas and bloating.) Pay attention to the places where you say or imply a **Should** and use Inquiry to accept reality on its own terms.

Fishing for Trouble

A school of fishy words that lead people
towards confusion and upset.

An unquestioned mind is the world of suffering.

—Byron Katie

Certain words consistently lead us down an emotional sinkhole. It's important to keep my ear out for them so I can prevent my clients from drowning in the despair these words create. We've already tasted the troublesome effects of the fattest **Fishing for Trouble** culprit: **Should**. Now we'll explore other dark waters of language.

Tanya had designed a life path for herself that was not only different from what her family expected but out of the box compared to society in general. Being so divergent made Tanya feel uncomfortable, and she sought frequent reassurance that the choices she was making were acceptable. The conversation below is full of **Fishing for Trouble** words highlighted in bold:

Tanya: My dad doesn't understand that I don't want to go to college.

Chana: And that upsets you?

Tanya: Yeah, I mean, isn't it **understandable** that after age 18 I'd want to make my own choices?

Tanya wants to feel supported in her thinking, despite it making her upset. This question shows she'd rather be justified than happy. Her emotional health demands that she be less interested in what is **understandable** and more interested in what is beneficial. My first step is to attempt to reword her statement into a belief we can inquire about:

Chana: You believe your father **should** support your choices now that you're 18?

Tanya: Yes! Exactly. He totally should.

71

Chana: And how do you react when you believe he should support you?

Tanya: I get so angry. My skin turns hot, and my fists clench. But doesn't it **make sense** that I should be angry? Isn't it **logical** to feel that way?

Tanya's back to wanting justification, now for her emotions rather than her beliefs. The problem is that her feelings aren't supporting the happiness she *really* wants, and it doesn't serve her to try to back them up with bigger bait. Again, the question is not whether her emotions are justified, but whether they get her where she wants to go. Other **Fishing for Trouble** words that fit the "justification" rubric, including: **fair**, **justified**, and **reasonable**.

Chana: What else comes up when you believe the thought that your father should support your choices?

Tanya: I start thinking about how I'm not old **enough**, smart **enough**, or knowledgeable **enough** to make decisions without his support.

Tanya's shared three additional beliefs she hasn't mentioned before, so let's add them to her **Thought Bank**:

> *I'm not old enough to make decisions on my own.*
>
> *I'm not smart enough to make decisions on my own.*
>
> *I'm not knowledgeable enough to make decisions on my own.*

She's also using another **Fishing for Trouble** word: **enough**. Another way to say enough is, "as it **should** be." The assumption is that we know exactly how much talent or height or beauty is ideal and that we have the capacity to assess whether we fit that rubric. The word **enough** always leads to sadness and frustration. Why? Because it forces us to step outside of ourselves and to be the ultimate, all-knowing judge of ourselves and our situation. Now, back to our regularly scheduled Inquiry.

Chana: What are you not able to do when you believe that your father should support your choices?

Tanya: It's hard to think straight. Like, I'm thinking of signing up for a computer programming course, and my mind goes all blurry every time I go to the computer school's website.

Chana: Can you think of a peaceful reason to keep the thought that your father should support your choices?

Tanya: Yeah. I **deserve** his support. I mean, I'm his daughter.

KABOOM! **Deserve** is a bomb of a word. Again, Tanya wants to feel justified in her desire for support while at the same time elevating it to the status of *Rule of the Universe*: All fathers **should** always support their daughters' decisions. In other words, she's saying she **should** get his support because *she **should** get his support*. This is circular, self-destructive thinking at its best. Notice I've asked Tanya to offer a peaceful reason her father should support her, yet her answer is presumably a stressful one.

Chana: Does it bring you peace to think that?

Tanya: Uh… peace?

Chana: Yes. How do you feel when you believe you **deserve** his support?

Tanya: Annoyed. Pissed off.

Chana: So, not peaceful.

Tanya: I guess not. No.

Chana: Can you think of a peaceful reason to keep the thought that your father should support you?

Tanya: … nah. But it's not **fair**. He's my dad. He says he loves me and wants me to be happy but then gets all flustered when I say I don't want to go to college.

When Tanya says, "It's not **fair**," she's arguing with reality. In other words, "If reality got it right, according to my accounting of how things **should** be, then my dad would support me." **Fair** is **Deserve's** best friend. They're different ways of saying **should**. That's why they're all **Fishing for Trouble** words – they all bait us into an ice hole of despair.

Chana: I hear a couple of thoughts we may want to add to your **Thought Bank**. Let me know if you believe them to be true.

Tanya: Okay.

Chana: You believe that dads should support their daughters.

Tanya: Yeah.

Now I walk up to the **ATM**.

Chana: And if your dad loves you, that means he should support your desire to skip college.

Tanya: Totally.

Chana: And if your dad says he wants you to be happy, that means that he should support all your choices.

Tanya: Shouldn't he?

Chana: What's the reality of it?

Tanya: He doesn't always.

Chana: How do you react when you believe that if your dad says he wants to you be happy it means that he should support your choices, and he doesn't?

Tanya: I get really mad at him. I don't want to talk to him.

Chana: And who would you be, trying to register for a programming course, without the thought?

Tanya: I could just read the info about each class. It would be so much easier to pick the one I want to take.

Chana: Anything else?

Tanya: I would feel calm.

Chana: Yes. Sit in that for a minute. Feel that calm. That's what you were hoping to feel when you wanted your father to support you.

Tanya: Yeah. I just wanted to feel like everything was going to be okay.

Chana: Exactly. But you can feel that way on your own, whether or not your father supports you. Feel that. You just created that feeling.

Tanya: It feels good.

Chana: And how are you around your father without the thought that he should support you?

Tanya: I can simply be with him. I can let myself laugh. Dad is very funny.

Chana: Wonderful. Now, let's turn it around. *Your father should support you* – what's the opposite of that?

Tanya: My father shouldn't support me.

Chana: Give me three reasons why that's true.

Tanya: He doesn't always.

Chana: Yes. What else?

Tanya: In his experience, college is the path towards success, and he wants me to be successful and financially stable. He thinks that'll make me happy.

Chana: And another reason?

Tanya: Sometimes I do stupid things. I wouldn't want him supporting that. I'd prefer he push me to think through some of my choices.

Chana: Can you give me another turnaround? One that starts with *you*.

Tanya: I should support me. Ooh. That's tough.

Chana: But you thought it was so easy for your dad.

Tanya: Touché.

Chana: Can you give me three reasons this thought is as true or truer than your original belief?

Tanya: Yeah. I'm the one who has to live with myself. And my choices. And whatever comes of them.

Chana: Good. Two more.

Tanya: I often doubt myself even when my dad *is* supportive. I could learn from him, sometimes.

Chana: Wow. What else?

Tanya: Um…. I can't think of anything else….

To help Tanya, let's introduce her to one of my friends, the pre-schooler. His words can help her see her mental processing a bit more clearly.

Chana: Let's say that a four-year-old passed by you on the street and said, "I think it's so fantastic that you're not going to college, Tanya. You're a superstar. I support every choice you make!" What would you think?

Tanya: I don't know. He's a kid. And doesn't know anything. I don't care what he thinks.

Chana: You don't feel more supported by his words?

Tanya: No way.

Chana: So you told yourself a story about this child and based on your story, you decided whether to support yourself with his words or not.

Tanya: Huh. Yeah, I guess I did.

Chana: And if your father were to say those words then you'd pat yourself on the back with them and hug yourself with them and fill your heart with them.

Tanya: (laughing) Probably!

Chana: So who supports you?

Tanya: I do! I get it! I should support myself. I should say things to myself that are supportive and take in others' words that are supportive, blocking out what's not. I like that.

In summary, Tanya's desire for the unfailing support of her father got in the way of her being happy with her own choices. By identifying the **Fishing For Trouble** words in her speech, she was able to get out of her own way and find better fish to fry.

Fishing For Trouble words trap us in upset and despair. Identifying these words and the havoc they wreak can help you move them out of the way and get closer to clarity and peace.

Monsters Under the Bed

The fearful beliefs underlying our
seemingly uncharged thinking.

I used to always say, 'Why me? Why don't I have a father? Why isn't he around? Why did he leave my mother?' But as I got older I looked deeper and thought, 'I don't know what my father was going through, but if he was around all the time, would I be who I am today?'

—LeBron James

Sometimes our greatest fears are hiding under what we believe to be grounded, logical, or supportive arguments. One way to get in touch with the root of the issue is to shine a flashlight under all that solidity and see what's lurking beneath the boxspring. That's just what Jack needed. He wanted to get married, but experienced a lot of blocks when it came to dating:

Jack: I can't seem to meet a woman I like.

Chana: Why?

Jack: I work on a construction site. Not exactly Ladies Central…

Chana: Is that the only place you spend your time?

Jack: Mostly.

Chana: Why?

Jack: I don't get out much.

Chana: Why is that?

Jack: I like being on my own.

On his own? This statement contradicts his original desire for companionship and hints to a **Monster Under the Bed.** It's time to turn on the flashlight and ask Jack about his fears.

Chana: **What do you think would happen if** you got out?

If I'm wrong here and Jack had a preference rather than a fear, he'll let me know. In this case, my gut feeling is spot on:

Jack: I don't know. I... I don't know how to act at parties and stuff.

Chana: Why?

Jack: I'll say something dumb, or lame, or just totally off.

Chana: **What do you think would happen** if you *didn't believe* that you'd say something totally off?

Jack: I might say what's on my mind. I wouldn't be careful. And then I'd make a total fool of myself.

Chana: So if you don't believe that you might say something off, then you'll say something off?

Jack: Yeah. It... protects me.

Chana: How do you react when you believe that you'll say something off?

Jack: I get jittery. I get super self-conscious.

Chana: And how do you act around women when you believe the thought?

Jack: It's hard for me to concentrate on what they're saying. I'm just too focused on what I'm going to say or when I should laugh or smile or something.

Chana: And then what happens?

Jack: I end up saying stuff that's totally off cause I'm not listening so well, so I'm not in tune to what's going on. I become too self-conscious.... Oh! I get it! When I think that thought, I get *more* off. Not *less*. *Whoa!* But...

Chana: But...?

Jack: But it's hard not to be self-conscious. I don't want to say something dumb.

Chana: What do you mean by "dumb?"

Jack: Like if I got a fact wrong.

Chana: **What are you afraid would happen** if you got a fact wrong?

Jack: That girls would laugh at me. I know they wouldn't be rude enough to do it out loud, but they would be – on the inside – cracking up.

Chana: **What are you afraid would happen** if they laughed?

Jack: That would be so humiliating!

Chana: And **what are you afraid would happen** if you were humiliated?

Jack: Then no one would want to have anything to do with me.

Chana: **What are you afraid would happen** if no one wanted to have anything to do with you?

Jack: I'd be all alone.

Now, let's walk up to the **ATM**.

Chana: What would it **mean** if you were all alone?

Jack: That I'm absolutely unlovable. Worthless.

Jack's *real* fear is that if he puts himself out there socially, he'll be exposing himself to experiences that would prove the underlying belief that he's unlovable. We could work on visualizing him going to parties, practice asking girls out, and disproving his concern that people would laugh at him, but it wouldn't uproot the fear of unworthiness lurking under the surface. So, let's go right for the **Monster** with our own claws unsheathed.

Chana: What feels the most painful: the belief that you're unlovable or that you're worthless?

Jack: That I'm worthless.

Chana: So. You're worthless. Is it true?

Jack: When you put it that way... it sounds less true.

Chana: So not a certain, "yes?"

Jack: Yeah.

Chana: And how do you react when you believe the thought that you're worthless?

Jack: My body collapses. I feel drained.

Chana: What else?

Jack: I feel like a hole wants to suck me into the ground.

Chana: What comes up for you emotionally?

Jack: I feel really sad. Just want to curl up into a ball and cry.

Chana: What are you unable to do when you believe the thought that you're worthless?

Jack: I can't think straight. I don't want to talk to anyone. Definitely don't want to go to a social event. For sure not. I just want to disappear.

Chana: Now. Take a deep breath and clear the air. Good. Imagine you're thinking of going to a party and the thought that you're worthless isn't there. Who would you be without the thought?

Jack: Oh. I just think about who might be there and whether I want to hang out with them or not. I can also feel if I have energy or if I'm tired. I'm more open to asking what's good for me. There's not all this tightness and pressure around the whole thing. It's simpler. Do I feel like going or not?

Chana: So let's turn it around. You're worthless. What's the opposite?

Jack: I'm not worthless.

Chana: Yes. Tell me how that's as true or truer than the original belief.

Jack: I have a number of friends who like hanging out with me even though I can be an awkward hermit at times.

Chana: What else?

Jack: I love my family, and they love me.

Chana: Feel that. Doesn't sound so worthless, does it?

Jack: No. They'd actually be sad if I disappeared.

Chana: Yes. Tell me another reason you're not worthless.

Jack: I'm a fantastic architect. My clients really appreciate how I find creative ways to design what they want and more.

Chana: Beautiful. Another one?

Jack: I volunteer at a soup kitchen. The people there really appreciate it.

Chana: And how about another turnaround.

Jack: I'm worthy?

Chana: Yes.

Jack: Um… My parents fed and housed me growing up. So I guess they thought that was worthwhile.

Chana: And how about now?

Jack: They continue to invest in me, I guess. I mean they don't give me money anymore because I support myself, but they offer advice and time and love.

Chana: They don't think they're wasting their time and resources.

Jack: No. It's not like a guilt trip for them. They seem to be happy to have me over and ask me about my life. And they keep nudging me about dating – they want me to be happy. They know I don't want to be alone.

Chana: What's another reason that you're worthy?

Jack: Uhh… I don't know. I'm stuck here.

Chana: Okay. Try this: who defines a person's worth?

Jack: I dunno. I guess every person is different. They can't all be measured the same way. I don't know if I could say exactly the worth of a kid or someone who's blind or handicapped. I guess even someone young and healthy like me. I don't really know what makes me worthy of existence. Now that I stop to think about it, I have no clue. I guess only G-d could know that.

Chana: And is your heart still beating?

Jack: Yes.

Chana: Who's making that happen?

Jack: Not me.

Chana: Did you turn it on this morning?

Jack: No. I didn't turn it on. I can't just turn it off, either.

Chana: So who does?

Jack: G-d, I guess. Oh! I get it! G-d is keeping my heart beating. So I *must* be worthy of existence.

Chana: Yes.

Jack: But wait. That sounds too simple.

Chana: Does it?

Jack: Hmm… Maybe I just made it complicated.

Chana: Perhaps. Who decided that you weren't worthy?

Jack: It felt like everyone was telling me that when I was a kid.

Chana: Did they actually *tell you* that?

Jack: (Pauses to think.) No. I guess I just thought that's what they meant. Like I had to earn my keep.

Chana: And meanwhile….

Jack: My heart's been beating the whole time.

Chana: Did you have to "earn" that?

Jack: Can't be. It beat even when I was a baby. And I couldn't earn anything back then. I was just a whining, pooping blob!

Chana: So can you know with complete certainty that you have to "earn" it now?

Jack: No. I can't know that. Maybe there's no such thing as earning it at all.

Chana: How does it feel when you believe the thought that your existence doesn't have to be earned?

Jack: Like a million bricks have just rolled off my back. It's such a relief. I feel like I can breathe.

Chana: And how would it feel to go to a party believing that you don't have to earn your worth?

Jack: I could just be there. And talk to people. Or not. Either way, it's okay. Thank you. This feels very good!

By directly asking Jack about his fears, we were able to discover his **Monsters Under the Bed**. In the light, Jack faced his subconscious assumptions about his worthiness, was able to question their validity, and chose a kinder perspective for himself.

Use the **Monsters Under the Bed** technique when your language implies fears lurking under the surface. Trust that when you ask, "what are you afraid would happen if…" answers will come bubbling to the surface. These answers can build a meaningful **Thought Bank** to kickstart pivotal change.

Download a **Monsters Under the Bed** worksheet from the **Free Bonus Section** of my website:

Hold.ChanaMason.com/bonus.

Caught up in Dramatics

Using strong language for dramatic effect
that ends up causing undue stress.

I never did give anybody hell.
I just told the truth, and they thought it was hell.

- Harry S Truman

W e all use our imaginative capacity to distort reality. This ability allows us to play with language and convey meaning beyond the simple facts. When I tell you, for example, that my heart is busting out of my chest, you know not to call an ambulance. Being able to use metaphor and imagery makes communication richer, but when this faculty is not entirely in our control, we can get **Caught Up in Dramatics** that may feel exciting, but can quickly overwhelm us.

Randy was often stressed out or depressed and didn't know how to get out of her funks:

Chana: What's upsetting you?

Randy: I hate my job.

Chana: What about it don't you like?

Randy: The commute is unbearable.

Right away, Randy is using strong language, which creates a strong physiological response in her body. Her muscles tense, her eyes roll, and her face flushes. Let's question whether she can't "bear" something she's been bearing for a while:

Chana: Is it true that you can't bear the commute?

Randy: Yeah. I hate it.

Chana: I hear you don't like it. But is it true that you can't bear it?

Randy: Yeah. I don't want to be on that bus.

Chana: You'd prefer not to be there. Does that mean you can't bear it?

Randy: Why do you keep asking that?

Chana: Take a moment to think over my question. Does the fact that you don't enjoy the bus mean you can't bear it?

Randy: Huh. I guess not.

Chana: And how do you react when you believe you can't bear it?

Randy: I get all tight. I don't want to talk to anyone or look at anyone.

Chana: Take a deep breath. Imagine yourself sitting on the bus without the thought that you can't bear the commute. How would you be without it?

Randy: I can't imagine that. It's like an oven on that bus. And we're packed like sardines. There's a guy who gets on at the stop after mine who always smells like sour garbage.

Two challenges have come up. One is that Randy has left Inquiry to go back into her story and build up evidence for her belief. The other is that she's **Caught Up in Dramatics**. Her metaphors serve to turn up the volume on her suffering and similarly increase her stress response. Top British therapist Marisa Peer says that dramatic language is quite pernicious because our subconscious takes it seriously. When we say something is "a headache," it might well lead us to get a headache. So too with experiences we label "a pain in the butt," "horrifying," or beyond our capacity to "handle." Randy's dramatic language leads her to feel panicky, tired, and upset. We'll need to reel her back in:

Chana: I see that you've left Inquiry and trailed back into your story. Take a few breaths and relax. Let's explore, just for a moment, how you would be without the thought that you can't bear the commute?

Randy: Hmm…

Chana: Are you okay?

Randy: Yeah, I guess.

Chana: Are you on the bus?

Randy: Yes.

Chana: And it's moving.

Randy: Of course.

Chana: So you're bearing the ride.

Randy: Oh. I am.

Chana: How do you know it's true that you can bear the ride?

Randy: Sometimes I bring a book on the bus and read it during the ride. I can get so caught up in the story; I forget I'm even on the bus!

Chana: What else?

Randy: I could get off the bus if I want to, but I choose to stay on.

Chana: And...

Randy: And I'm still alive when I get off.

Let's highlight other ways Randy has gotten **Caught Up in Dramatics** so she can further understand her language patterns:

Chana: Keep your eyes closed and watch yourself sitting on the bus. Notice what happens to you when you believe it's like an oven, and you're packed like sardines.

Randy: Uch. Right away I cringe. I feel trapped. Like I can't breathe.

Chana: Is it true that the bus is like an oven?

Randy: Sure!

Chana: I hear you believe it's like an oven. But is it *actually* true?

Randy: It's hot but... No. Not *really* like an oven.

Chana: Why do you describe it that way?

Randy: Um. I don't know.

Chana: How does it serve you to describe the bus as being like an oven?

Randy: I feel kind of a rush. I feel powerful somehow.

Chana: This rush… does it feel peaceful?

Randy: No. It's quite stressful. Anxious. Oh!

Chana: Why did you say, "Oh?"

Randy: I just realized… a lot of the time when I feel anxious, it's exactly like this.

Chana: Exactly like what?

Randy: This same rush. This same stress.

Chana: What would you prefer?

Randy: To feel relaxed. To go with the flow more.

Chana: And how could you do that?

Randy: It's like with the bus. I'm already on it anyhow, so I might as well accept that I'm not getting off. I don't have to make it such a drama. I don't have to fight it so much.

Chana: What could you do if you weren't fighting it?

Randy: I'd have space to think. Maybe even to use the commute time to look for a job I like more.

Chana: You'd like to leave your job.

Randy: Yeah. I mean, I think so. But now I wonder if I'm maybe just blowing the things I don't like out of proportion. Can we look at that next?

Chana: Sure. You said you hate your job. Is that still true?

Randy: I think so.

Chana: Why?

Randy: Well, first off, the hours are horrific. I have to wake up ridiculously early every morning to get there on time.

Randy's back to her superlatives. Let's show this drama queen her day-to-day isn't Shakespeare:

Chana: The hours are horrific, is it true?

Randy: Yes.

Chana: How do you react when you believe that?

Randy: Tight. And… that same rush again.

Chana: Who would you be, standing at the counter without the thought that the hours are horrific?

Randy: I'd just be serving people. Same as before… only different. I'd be more present. I think I'd notice people more. Gosh.

Chana: Gosh?

Randy: Yeah. I don't think I've ever really paid attention to any of my customers. I was too busy hating my job.

Chana: How do you feel?

Randy: All funny inside. I think part of why I hated my job was because I felt so lonely. But that's because I never connected with anyone. It's hard to do that when you're pissed off.

Chana: Then is it the hours or your story about them that makes you lonely?

Randy: My story. For sure.

Chana: Let's try and turn it around. What's the opposite of "your hours are horrific?"

Randy: My hours are *not* horrific.

Chana: How is that true?

Randy: I get to work when it's daylight. So I don't have to mess up my body clock or anything.

Chana: What else?

Randy: Okay. This one is kind of embarrassing. Don't laugh, okay?

Chana: Alright.

Randy: I don't have to commute during rush hour, so my bus ride is actually shorter.

Chana: Good to notice. Any other reason your hours aren't horrific?

Randy: Horrific is a strong word and belongs in a scary movie. There's really nothing horrifying about working 7-3. It's actually pretty dull and predictable.

Chana: How does it feel to have dull and predictable hours?

Randy: No rush.

Chana: Less exciting?

Randy: Yes. But also more relaxing. I'd rather reserve excitement for the movies.

Extreme words and metaphors can make life feel thrilling and give us an adrenaline rush, but they can also block our ability to be present, see clearly, and think calmly. During our dialogues, Randy learned to pay more attention to her word choices and their effects on her physiological and emotional experience. She gained clarity on what she enjoyed or disliked about her job and, from a centered place, decided to look elsewhere for employment.

People who are **Caught Up in Dramatics** learn from seeing the effect their language has on their story of reality and their subsequent reaction to it. It's important to identify these language traps so you can more consciously choose how you narrate the story of your life.

Double Bind Study

Looking closely at the links we've made between concepts and questioning the validity of those connections.

We are shaped by our thoughts; we become what we think. When the mind is pure, joy follows like a shadow that never leaves.

—Buddha

Do you remember Wendy from **The Survey**? She believed that "skinny people are shallow," which held her back from losing weight. Wendy was caught in a **Bind**, a situation in which no matter what she chose to do, she'd lose. If she met her weight goals, she'd have to suffer from being shallow and having little respect for herself. On the other hand, staying deep meant having to be obese and a pre-diabetic. Because both of these options were painful, it was easier to stay with the status quo. It was easier to continue the habits she had in place than attempt to climb the hurdle created by her fear of shallowness.

Greg came to my husband, Dave, and myself asking for business advice. He wanted to make more money but kept finding himself making less than he needed to live. Dave and I have learned over the years that someone's **Financial Blueprint** is a crucial indicator of their eventual financial and business success. The narratives we tell about ourselves, other people, and the world make up our **Blueprint**. Just as an architect's blueprint sets the parameters for what will become a building, our mental **Blueprint** defines the parameters of our lives. If, for example, our **Blueprint** includes the belief that the world is an unsafe place, we'll be less adventurous, trusting, and calm. If we believe that money never comes our way, studies have shown that we'll walk right past cash left on the sidewalk, not to mention other financial opportunities. We'll thus have less money in our pocket at the end of the day.

To assess Greg's **Financial Blueprint**, we asked him to fill out the *Millionaire Mind* **Survey** developed by T. Harv Eker, which presents an exhaustive list of limiting beliefs around money and success. The statement on which he scored the highest was, "Rich people are evil." Right away we knew Greg was caught in a

Bind of lose-lose. He either got to be good and poor or evil and wealthy. Neither of those options felt appealing. Greg didn't want to be a loser in the money game any longer, so we used Inquiry to question his thinking.

Chana: Can you absolutely know that rich people are evil?

Greg: Yeah. Just look at what's-his-face, that big stock market guy. He made off with so many people's money and got rich off little old ladies' pensions.

Chana: How do you react when you believe that rich people are evil?

Greg: I get frustrated. I boil up and want to punch somebody.

Chana: How do you feel in your body?

Greg: Tight. Everything is tight. And hot.

Chana: What are you unable to do when you believe rich people are evil?

Greg: I can't be in the present moment. I'm just thinking about rich people I've heard of screwing people over. My head becomes a newsreel.

Chana: Now close your eyes and imagine you're at your desk working on your business. You're talking to a customer and are focused on his needs.

Greg: Okay. I can see that.

Chana: Now watch what happens when the belief that rich people are evil pops in.

Greg: I feel limp. Tired. I don't want to write the email. I'll just push it off 'til tomorrow...

Chana: So why do you believe this thought that makes you limp?

Greg: Hmm... that's a good question. I don't want to be evil, but in that moment I'm not so nice. The customer is asking for help, and I'm blowing him off. That's not the kind of high consciousness behavior I'm hoping to engage in.

Chana: It sounds like you believe this thought will protect you from being an evil person.

Greg: I thought it would. But… Ouch.

Chana: Why did you say that?

Greg: I just pictured myself all lazy and limp and at the same time tight and angry. I don't think I've ever been a good person when I'm feeling like that. If anything, I become selfish and arrogant.

Chana: What do you want to do?

Greg: I'd like to think about this differently. I don't want to be angry.

Chana: What would be a different way?

Greg: I guess I could question whether rich people are evil.

Chana: What would be an alternative?

Greg: Rich people are good.

Chana: How is that true?

Greg: I don't know. I'm stuck.

Greg has built a robust neural pathway between two human qualities: Wealthy and Evil. Like all qualities, these two exist in different people in differing degrees. Some people are criminals with no wealth. Some use deceptive tactics to embezzle money. Others are swimming in cash and are great philanthropists and leaders. There are also, of course, homeless people who help others with the little they have. If you flip through your mental rolodex you'll find examples of all of these. I'm going to invite Greg to do the same.

Chana: Do you know any wealthy people personally?

Greg: Yes. Rick and Tommy.

Chana: Are they evil?

Greg: (laughs)

Chana: Why'd you laugh?

Greg: I know these guys. They've been my neighbors for years, yet somehow, in my head, I had to block them out in order to believe that rich people are evil.

Chana: Why is that?

Greg: Because they are the most generous guys I know. They're constantly giving to charity and offering their time to help others.

Chana: Can you give me another reason why rich people are good?

Greg: Yeah, actually. Rick is like a few people in town who's successful because of his business. He's gotten rich from it, but other people have benefitted too. Like Harry. He's been employed by Rick's laundry business for years and isn't just able to put food on the table, he's saving for retirement. Harry loves his job.

Chana: What's one more reason?

Greg: An image of Bill Gates just flashed through my head. I used to hate his guts because he was all high and mighty taking over the world with Microsoft, but then I saw his TED talk. He's dedicating billions of dollars and most of his time to curing malaria and educating people. That's pretty good.

Chana: Great. Can you give me another turnaround for rich people are evil?

Greg: Rich people aren't evil? Isn't that the same thing?

Chana: It sounds similar, but you might be surprised at the different perspectives your mind offers with a slight change in language.

Greg: Alright. Okay, I see one now.

Chana: What is that?

Greg: Well, there's being *good*, like giving charity or creating jobs. But there's also not being *evil*, which has to do with a person's character, like how they behave.

Chana: And how do you think rich people behave?

Greg: I guess I don't know. I honestly haven't stopped and thought of them as people.

Chana: Would you guess that business owners make more money from being honest and fair or by cheating and being evil?

Greg: I never thought of it that way.

Chana: Which way?

Greg: Well, I know that if I walk into a laundromat, say, like Rick's, and they were rude or charged me extra, I wouldn't go there anymore.

Chana: What does that mean to you?

Greg: I can't believe I'm saying this, but I can see you have to be pretty honest to make it in business. And nice, too.

Chana: How does that realization make you feel?

Greg: Good. Settled more. Calm. Like I'm more honest with myself. But now the thought of Enron popped into my head.

Chana: Why?

Greg: I guess I don't want to be caught unawares. They were super dishonest and messed with a lot of people.

Chana: Do you have to believe that rich people are evil to be aware?

Greg: No. I guess not. I could do my research before making an investment. But still. Enron is a big deal. They fooled even the experts.

Chana: Big deal how?

Greg: They were all over the news, and people talked about it for months.

Chana: Were they all over the news because rich people are evil?

Greg: Yes. Well, wait. Let me think about this. The news usually announces stuff that's surprising. If it was surprising what Enron did, then I guess it's unusual. Now that I think about it, you could probably get away with being sneaky for a while, but it'll eventually catch up with you as it did with Enron. In the long run, for people who care about the success of their business and their reputation, being a slime-ball is probably ineffective.

Chana: What do you want to do?

Greg: I don't want to be a slime-ball! I want to be a good, upstanding guy. And I want to build a successful business.

Chana: How might you go about that?

Greg: I think having principles on my wall would be helpful. I want to remember what's important to me.

Chana: Like what?

Greg: Honesty, Decency, Respect. Also, I want to guarantee my products because I want the customer to be happy. And I want to be fair to my employees and suppliers (sinks.)

Chana: Why did your posture change?

Greg: I haven't been paying them on time. That's not cool. I'm going to make that a principle: Pay everyone on time.

Chana: Anything else?

Greg: Yes, I want to grow as a person, and I want my business to be a vehicle for that.

Chana: How?

Greg: Hmm… through books and classes. I bet there are people out there who teach about how to grow a business on solid principles. I could read and watch them and share them with my staff.

Chana: How do you feel?

Greg: Strong. There's no anger left. I'm just excited to move forward.

Chana: Is there anything else you want to do?

Greg: Yes. Can we work through the rest of my bogus beliefs on this **Survey**?

Greg had subconsciously decided that it was infinitely better to be an upstanding person in debt than a slime-ball on financially solid footing. There was thus always too much month at the end of his money. By engaging in Inquiry, Greg was able to disentangle the connection he had built between Wealth and Evil and free himself to pursue both financial success and a high-conscious life.

We can get stuck in a **Bind** when we believe that two things we want are mutually exclusive and can trap ourselves into thinking that no matter what we do, we lose. Doing a **Double Bind Study** allows us to question the underlying logic of our beliefs and opens us up to new ways of thinking.

Dead Weight

Lugging around heavy meanings
to otherwise neutral terms.

> *"History is full of the dead weight of things which have escaped the control of the mind, yet drive man on with a blind force."*
>
> —F. M. Powicke

In the **Double Bind Study**, we got a chance to see how destructive it can be to intertwine two ideas together without thinking through the consequences of such a marriage of meanings. In this section, we'll be delving deeper into how our minds go about understanding the world and how we can catch ourselves from developing beliefs that wreak all sorts of havoc. Lucky for us, Greg was carrying around a whole lot of **Dead Weight**, giving us ample material to explore.

Chana: Are there any other beliefs in the survey that stand out for you?

Greg: Yeah. "If I ask for help, people will think I'm weak."

Chana: How highly did you identify with that one?

Greg: I scored a 9 out of 10.

Chana: I notice you clenching your eyes.

Greg: I'm embarrassed just thinking about it.

Chana: So if you need advice on how to build your business…?

Greg: I'd try to figure it out on my own.

Chana: And how has that been working for you?

Greg: I fumble a lot. I've learned so much the hard way.

Chana: You've had to; you're carrying around **Dead Weight**.

Greg: What do you mean?

Chana: You've equated seeking help with weakness.

Greg: It's another **Double Bind**. I can either get help and be weak or struggle on my own and be strong.

Chana: Exactly. You've got it.

Greg: So what's the **Dead Weight**?

Chana: It's a ball-and-chain you've attached to a word or concept. You know you're carrying around **Dead Weight** when something you desire is dragging around something you loathe. They're entangled with each other, which makes you feel twisted up inside.

Greg: Yes, that's exactly how I feel. Tight and nauseous.

Chana: So, when you believe that if you ask for help, people will think you're weak, what's the thing you desire?

Greg: If I were honest with myself, asking for help would probably lead me towards success much faster than doing it alone.

Chana: Exactly, help is your target. The **Dead Weight** is the thing *you're* avoiding.

Greg: Weakness.

Chana: The fear of weakness is so heavy, it keeps you from moving forward.

In **Neuro-Linguistic Programming (NLP)**, we talk about three ways the mind develops its *map* (story and beliefs about the self, life, and the universe) and processes the outside world.

We use **Generalizations** to quickly make sense of world.

It's helpful to assume that the round thing in front of the driver seat in my car will function *just like* the round thing in a rental car so that I don't have to rediscover the steering wheel every time I get into a vehicle. However, it can be destructive to use one negative experience with a man as the basis for the belief that "All men are jerks."

We use **Distortion** to alter reality to suit our beliefs.

I can walk into a run-down apartment and helpfully use distortion to imagine how it would look with some touch-ups and a new coat of paint. Conversely, I can also use this faculty to harmfully alter how I hear another person's offer for assistance as an attempt to manipulate me instead.

We use **Deletion** to filter out stimuli that don't serve our beliefs

As I focus on writing these words, it's important for me to ignore the rustling of leaves outside my window or the subtle temperature change brought on by my air conditioner. To my detriment, though, deletion might cause me to ignore a phone call from a new acquaintance if I believe that "No one wants to be my friend."

As we notice these processes at work, we can viscerally understand how our consciousness is creating its version of reality minute by minute. We cannot keep our minds from generalizing, distorting, and deleting information, lest we go mad. What we *can* do is examine the beliefs that make up our maps. As is true with all **Dead Weight** beliefs, Greg has used generalization to make a sweeping assumption about what it means to seek help. He probably developed this belief at a young age, before he ever had a chance to examine its wisdom. Since then, he's been distorting and deleting his experience of reality to only notice the people who have been weakened by the assistance of others, rather than strengthened by it.

Greg: It's hard for me to imagine how asking for help isn't weak though. Doesn't it mean there's something wrong with me?

Chana: I hear how strongly you believe that. It's why Inquiry is going to help you. I'm going to mirror your question back to you. Does asking for help mean there's something wrong with you?

Greg: Yes. It feels like it.

Chana: Now I'd like you to engage your intellect. Can you absolutely know that it's true that asking for help means you're weak?

Greg: I still want to say yes.

Chana: Thank you for your honesty. That's all we're seeking here. Now, how do you react when you believe that asking for help means there's something wrong with you?

Greg: Tight. I want to hide my face in my hands. I want to get small and hide.

Chana: What are you unable to do when you believe the thought?

Greg: I for sure can't ask for help. I think I get dumber, too. It's like I can't even ask myself for help. I don't feel so competent or resourceful. (Eyes pop up.)

Chana: Why did your eyes just pop up?

Greg: I just realized how weak I sound. It's like I'm already weak even without asking for help. I get so small from the fear of looking weak that it's hard to get anything done.

Chana: I think you're ready to offer alternatives to this belief. What's the opposite of asking for help means there's something wrong with you?

Greg: Asking for help means there's nothing wrong with me?

Chana: Yes. Give me three reasons that's true.

Greg: I made my best friend in college by asking this kid on the quad who was playing bongos to teach me how to play. He was so excited to share what he knew, and we bonded over it.

Chana: Two more.

Greg: Hmm…. I can't think of anything.

Chana: Do you ever hire an expert to do any of your work for you?

Greg: I hire an accountant to do my taxes. I guess that's seeking help. I never thought of it that way though.

Chana: Why not?

Greg: I guess what would mean admitting that I was getting help. Then I would never get an accountant, and I'd have really messed up tax filing.

Chana: So you made up a story that hiring an accountant is not "seeking help" so that you could still feel good about the decision.

Greg: Yeah. Oh. I just thought of something. My clients ask me for help all the time. It's why they hire me.

Chana: And do you think there's something wrong with them?

Greg: Actually, I think they're smart for hiring a consultant to do in a few hours what it would take them months to learn how to do. It just seems efficient.

Chana: So you help people for a living. You work with people who are seeking help all the time and -

Greg: And I never see them as weak for asking for help. I actually get annoyed with the ones who pretend to know more than they do and don't ask for clarification or assistance. Ha!

Chana: Why'd you laugh?

Greg: I just realized that asking for help doesn't make my clients weak; it makes them *strong!* I love working with the ones who ask clarifying questions and get the best results by applying what I teach them.

Chana: How do you feel?

Greg: Like twenty million bricks have just rolled off my shoulders. I've been hiding from experts like myself who are so eager to teach what they know, and I've held myself back so much!

Chana: What do you want to do?

Greg: I want to be real with people. I want to ask for help when I need it. But I also want to apply what I learn and make my teachers glad they invested in me.

Chana: Do you feel done with this topic?

Greg: Yes, thank you.

Chana: My pleasure.

Greg had woven together two concepts: seeking assistance and weakness. Asking for help is a neutral term; it doesn't mean anything other than what we choose to attach to it. Weakness became **Dead Weight** that didn't allow Greg to live freely and ask for the help that could have propelled him forward. As he let that old ball-and-chain go, he became free to seek assistance simply because he wanted it and saw the wisdom in learning from those more experienced than himself. Once he freed himself from the shackles of weakness, Greg became a voracious reader, enrolled in business and marketing courses, and hired a business coach to help take his consultancy to the next level.

When we've attached a negative meaning to something we need or want, we know we're carrying around **Dead Weight**. By questioning our thinking, we can disentangle the assumption that what we desire is wrong or unattainable, unshackle our **Dead Weight**, and free ourselves to ask, receive, and enjoy the blessings in store for us.

Reaction Contraction:
EXPERIENCING YOUR SUFFERING

You must take personal responsibility. You cannot change the circumstances, the seasons, or the wind, but you can change yourself. That is something you have charge of.

—Jim Rohn

Now that we've identified how beliefs and language can trip us up, it's time to take a look at how, precisely, our feelings and behaviors can lead us to the truth. If you're like me, you might find yourself swinging between emotions like a pendulum, not necessarily knowing how or why. Stopping to understand our emotional reactions to our thinking can help us shift our consciousness because every emotion you experience is the product of a thought. In this section, we're going to explore how it is that you respond to your thinking and how your reactions can guide you to know whether a thought is serving you or hurting you.

The Anatomy of Feedback

An understanding of how your physiology
and emotions respond to beliefs.

If you put your hand into a fire, does anyone have to
tell you to move it? Do you have to decide? No: When
your hand starts to burn, it moves. You don't have
to direct it; the hand moves itself. In the same way,
once you understand, through Inquiry, that an untrue
thought causes suffering, you move away from it.

—Byron Katie

Most people are unaware that they are not their thoughts. They don't recognize that their body and emotions are reacting to their thinking and that they can disentangle themselves from the beliefs that are causing their suffering. In my workshops, I like to give participants a visceral taste of what I call the **Anatomy of Feedback**: their unique physiological and psychological response to truth or falsehood.

When we believe what's true, our bodies manifest one type of experience; when we're attached to what is false, we manifest something completely different. Here is a basic script for an **Anatomy of Feedback** session. Take a moment to try it yourself:

ANATOMY OF FALSEHOOD

Close your eyes. Take three slow, deep breaths.

Think of a time you felt disconnected from yourself, others, and the world (the divine). Try to place yourself in that moment as vividly as you can. Turn up the volume on the sights, colors, sounds, and smells around you. Pay attention to how you feel in this moment.

> *How is your breathing? Deep or shallow?*
>
> *What is your heart rate?*
>
> *What does your posture want to do?*
>
> *Do your muscles feel tight or loose?*
>
> *What is going on in your chest?*

What do you feel in your stomach?

What thoughts go through your mind?

What emotions come up for you?

Take three more slow, deep breaths, open your eyes, and write down your answers.

You now have a distinct taste of how you react to **Falsehood**. I've done this with hundreds of people, and their responses all fit a similar pattern. They say they experience tightness in their body, anxious or violent thinking, and dark emotions. Now you have your unique **Anatomy of Falsehood** down on paper as a reference for the future.

ANATOMY OF TRUTH

Close your eyes again. Take three slow, deep breaths and clear your mind.

Think of a time you felt connected to yourself, others, and the world (the divine). Try to place yourself in that moment as vividly as you can. Turn up the volume on the sights, colors, sounds, and smells around you. Pay attention to how you feel in this moment.

How is your breathing? Deep or shallow?

What is your heart rate?

What does your posture want to do?

Do your muscles feel tight or loose?

What is going on in your chest?

What do you feel in your stomach?

What thoughts come up in your mind?

What emotions come up for you?

Take three more slow, deep breaths, open your eyes, and write down your answers [if you're facilitating someone else, repeat each question one by one].

How was it to react to **Truth**? It usually manifests as openness and lightness in the body, clarity of thought, and bright emotions. You've got your **Anatomy of Truth** on paper now as well.

The **Anatomy of Feedback** is essential to Inquiry. Recognizing your response to **Truth** and **Falsehood** will prove invaluable when determining whether or not a thought is helpful or harmful to you, making your path towards living a harmonious and joyous life all the easier.

> Use the **Anatomy of Feedback** if you're unaware of your psychological or physiological response to stressful thoughts. This tool is also a great way to begin a relationship with a new client or group workshop to help people quickly learn that their physiology and emotions can tell them a lot about their thinking.

Download an **Anatomy of Feedback** worksheet from the **Free Bonus Section** of my website:

Hold.ChanaMason.com/bonus.

The Experience Buffet

A collection of questions that flesh out
a person's varied psychological and
physiological reactions to a thought.

It is the mark of an educated mind to be able to
entertain a thought without accepting it.

—*Aristotle*

I love how Inquiry easily helps us separate truth from fiction, joy from pain, and perceived experience from objective reality. We experience this distinction most when contrasting our reactions to believing a thought and to living without it. When we ask, "How do you react when you believe that thought?" we viscerally taste the suffering a belief is creating in our lives. Other questions reveal even deeper layers of our reactions.

Like a party buffet, an **Experience Buffet** of sub-questions brings out unique and specific flavors of a particular thought. In the dialogue below, you'll see many of the "dishes" in the **Experience Buffet** in action. I've compiled an exhaustive list of the questions at the end of this chapter.

Toni harbored tremendous resentment towards a roommate she had in college. Years had already passed, but Toni's anger had barely abated. She wasn't clear exactly why she was angry, so I asked her to **Rant**.

Toni: There were four of us, including Zoe. When we first signed on the apartment, we wrote up a list of house rules. We were supposed to take turns cleaning the kitchen, bathroom, and shared spaces. Also, we had to buy supplies like toilet paper and soap and stuff. Plus the landlord stipulated that we pay our rent by the 1st of the month. A month into the year, Zoe broke up with her boyfriend. She was a total emotional wreck, so we gave her a lot of room to be upset and mourn. But the next month she didn't have her rent ready by the 1st. The rest of us had to pitch in to compensate, which meant I couldn't go out for coffee or dinner until she finally paid us back, which wasn't till the 15th. But it was hard to be mad since she was so upset. We gave her some more slack. The three of us picked up her laundry in the living room and did her dishes and cleaned the frickin' toilet when it was her turn. That sucked! But we figured we'd want someone to help *us* out if we were having a hard time. Come second semester, not much had changed. She left a mess everywhere, and it was so disgusting! My other roommates got so sick of it. They just wanted to kick her out.

Chana: So did you?

Toni: No. How could we? She had nowhere to go and... I mean, she thought she was going to *marry* this guy. I didn't want to be insensitive.

Can you guess the beliefs lingering underneath Toni's **Rant**? I'd like you to stop reading, take out pen and paper, and write all the troubling thoughts you assume Toni's believing, either because she's said them outright or hinted at them between the lines. Once you finish, take a look at what I've written on my notepad:

Zoe should have cleaned the kitchen, bath, etc.

Zoe should have paid her rent on time.

She should have shared equal responsibility in the apartment.

She should have followed the rules.

We should not have had to pay her late rent.

I should not have had to clean up after her mess.

I couldn't kick her out.

She had nowhere to go.

If I kicked her out, I would have been really insensitive to her.

She should have been more respectful.

I could read the list to Toni, but I want to see if she can identify her most bothersome belief outright.

Chana: What about this situation upsets you the most?

Toni: That she didn't respect me. It was so not cool.

Chana: That sounds like the perfect place to start. Can you think of a specific time when you harbored the belief that she didn't respect you?

Toni: Um…. yeah. There was a day that I had a date with this guy I really liked. I invited him over, and her stuff was all over the couch and her dishes from two nights before were rotting in the sink. It was so gross.

Chana: And at that moment, you're believing the thought, "She doesn't respect me."

Toni: Yes!

Chana: Can you absolutely know that she doesn't respect you?

Toni: Yeah. It's so obvious.

Chana: **How do you react when you believe that?**

Toni: I want to punch her. I get very pissed.

Chana: **How do you feel, in your body**, when you believe she doesn't respect you?

Toni: Everything gets all tight. My chest gets red hot. My fists clench. I want to scream.

Chana: **What are you afraid would happen if you didn't believe she doesn't respect you**? (**Monsters Under the Bed**)

Toni: Then I'd be a total pushover. I wouldn't stick up for myself.

Chana: So if you didn't believe it, you'd be a pushover? Is that true?

Toni: Oh. No, actually. I was a total pushover then. I didn't stick up for myself *at all*.

Chana: So believing the thought….

Toni: Made me do the stuff that I was hoping to avoid! That sucks!

Chana: Yes. And, in that moment, **how do you treat yourself when you believe that she doesn't respect you**?

Toni: Oh. I don't take care of myself. I'm too busy fuming. I'm so embarrassed and humiliated in front of this guy and embarrassed that I'm mad.

Chana: **And how do you treat her**?

Toni: I avoid her, can't look her in the eye. Or I'm too nice to her because I feel bad.

Chana: **And what are you not able to do when you believe that she doesn't respect you**?

Toni: I can't think straight. I can't be calm. I'm just fuming.

Chana: **Can you see a peaceful reason to keep the thought**?

Toni: No. I get mad even at the hint of the thought.

Chana: Now, take a deep breath and clear the air. Close your eyes and imagine yourself in your apartment with her dishes in the sink and her stuff on the couch. How are you without the thought that she doesn't respect you?

Toni: I'm calmer. I can quickly pick up the stuff on the couch and throw it into Zoe's room. And it's not that embarrassing with the guy. Let's get real; I'm sure his apartment is a pig sty.

Chana: So, let's turn it around. Zoe doesn't respect you. What's the 180 degree opposite of that?

Toni: Zoe… is not so bad?

Chana: We're not trying to get all sophisticated with turnarounds. Let's use simple language. What's the opposite of, "Zoe doesn't respect you."

Toni: Zoe does respect me?

Chana: That's it. Now give me three reasons why that's true.

Toni: She wanted to keep living with me. And as far as I know, she didn't gossip about me.

Chana: What else?

Toni: She invited me to her wedding a couple of years ago. And she sent me a holiday card in December. I guess I just assumed she didn't respect me. But why else wouldn't she follow the rules?

Chana: Have you asked her?

Toni: No, I haven't. I actually have no idea what she was thinking.

Chana: How do you feel?

Toni: Embarrassed.

Chana: Why?

Toni: I made assumptions about her and judged her for them.

Chana: Why do you feel embarrassed about that?

Toni: Because I want to be more thoughtful than that.

Chana: Do you have to feel embarrassed to be that way?

Toni: I think so…

Chana: Well, how do you behave when you feel embarrassed?

Toni: I want to hide. I don't want to talk to anyone. I for sure don't want to call Zoe.

Chana: Does feeling embarrassed help you be more thoughtful?

Toni: Oh, no. Totally the opposite. I think I'd rather be thoughtful. I should call Zoe and apologize. I could also ask her why she behaved the way she did and tell her how I felt about it. That would clear the air, and we could be friends without this hairy elephant in the room.

Chana: In the meantime, let's turn this thought around again. What's another opposite of she doesn't respect you? Try changing the subject of the statement.

Toni: I don't respect me?

Chana: Yes. How's that true?

Toni: Um. I'm not always so kind to myself. Like… I enjoy a neat room, but I often don't make my bed or will let my laundry pile up in the corner. And in my head sometimes I call myself dumb, or stupid, or forgetful.

Chana: Let's focus on the situation in the apartment. How else did you not respect yourself?

Toni: I don't know.

Chana: It seems the rules of the apartment were important to you.

Toni: Yes.

Chana: Did you respect them?

Toni: For sure I did! I always cleaned up and paid on time.

Chana: And what about Zoe?

Toni: She didn't keep to the rules at all.

Chana: And you enabled her to continue to do that.

Toni: Yes. Oh. That's how *I* didn't keep the rules. I let *her* break them. So I didn't respect the rules. I didn't respect something that was important to me.

Chana: **What were you afraid would happen if you upheld the rules? (Monsters)**

Toni: I'd have to kick her out.

Chana: And **what were you afraid would happen if you kicked her out**?

Toni: She'd hate me! She'd think I was horrible.

Chana: **And that would mean...? (ATM)**

Toni: Maybe that I'm a bad person.

Chana: So if you kicked Zoe out it would have meant that you're a bad person?

Toni: Oh. No. That doesn't make sense.

Chana: What else could it mean?

Toni: It could just mean that breaking rules has consequences.

Chana: Yes.

Toni: Could it really be that simple?

Chana: What do you think?

Toni: I guess it could. If I don't pay my taxes or stop at a light, I get fined. The truth is, if we hadn't covered for her, our landlord would have kicked us all out. But actually, it was her fault!

Chana: So what does that teach you about your life now?

Toni: Sometimes I don't stand up for what's important to me because I'm trying to be nice. But really I'm not respecting myself, and then I get resentful and blame everyone else for not taking care of my rules.

Chana: Whose job is that?

Toni: Totally mine!

Below is the **Experience Buffet**, a list of questions gleaned from Byron Katie's recorded and written dialogues. Like with a brunch buffet, you get to choose which questions will be your bread and butter and which ones you might use as occasional toppings. There's no right or wrong amount of questions. The more you ask, the deeper your understanding will be. Use whatever is comfortable and appropriate for the situation.

Note that not all questions are relevant to the Inquiry at hand, so asking *more* may even be *less*, by distracting or confusing you. Be creative and flexible, have fun, and remember to hold a safe space for your reactions to the thought. With any luck, you'll have a full belly and a loose belt by the end of the meal!

a. What images do you see, past and future, when you believe the thought?

b. What physical sensations arise as you think the thought and witness those images?

c. What emotions arise when you believe the thought?

d. Whose business are you in when you believe the thought? (See **There's No Business Like Your Business**)

e. When was the first time you remember believing the thought? (See **The Time Machine**)

f.   Do any obsessions or addictions begin to appear when you believe the thought? (See **The Addiction Loop and Aggression Tailspin**)

g.   How do you treat the person(s) in this situation when you believe the thought?

h.   How do you treat yourself when you believe the thought?

i.   Can you see a reason to drop the thought?

j.   Can you find one peaceful reason to keep the thought?

k.   What are you afraid would happen if you didn't believe the thought? (More **Monsters Under the Bed** to inquire about.)

l.   How do you/your ego/personality gain from believing the thought?

m.   What are you not able to do or see when you believe the thought?

n.   Does the thought bring peace or stress into your life?

Use the **Experience Buffet** when you want a deep understanding of a given thought in all its varied manifestations.

Download an **Experience Buffet** worksheet from
the **Free Bonus Section** of my website:
Hold.ChanaMason.com/bonus.

The Time Machine

Facilitating Inquiry with your younger self,
who developed a belief now held dear.

The world doesn't make sense.
We make sense of the world.

—*Barry Neil Kaufman*

D o you remember Melanie? In **Just Desserts**, I asked her to write a list of reasons she felt she deserved the "loser" guys she was dating and another list of why she didn't deserve a "winner." In the second list, she wrote that she was scared she'd take advantage of a "good" guy. Having already worked with Melanie for a couple of months, it was clear to me that she was thoughtful, considerate, and kind. She was the last person I would imagine taking advantage of someone. It was a far cry from her character.

I asked her what about her behavior made her feel this way about herself, and she said that it didn't match her behavior; she just *felt* this way. Basic Inquiry wouldn't help her, because she already thought the belief was illogical. Nonetheless, she couldn't shake it. Because this belief was so out of touch with her current reality, my instincts told me that it was formed earlier in Melanie's life.

Just like a scrape can leave a permanent scar on our knee, a belief formed at a less conscious moment in our lives can stick with us permanently. To heal that "thought scar," I find it useful to go back to that moment and question the logic of that younger self. I thus invited Melanie to step into **The Time Machine**. She closed her eyes, breathed slowly, and relaxed. I encouraged her to trust whatever memory would come up when I asked her:

Chana: When was the first time you remember believing that you might take advantage of someone?

Melanie: I'm seven. In my dad's house. It's just him and me. I'm at the kitchen table doing homework, and he's at the stove cooking dinner.

Chana: And you believe you might take advantage of someone?

127

Melanie: Yes. I'm taking advantage of my dad.

Chana: How?

Melanie: He's making dinner. I'm not making it. I'm not helping him.

Chana: Is he saying anything about you taking advantage of him?

Melanie: No. But it *feels* like I am.

By asking, "When was the first time you remember believing this thought?" I nudge Melanie into a more formative time: in this case when she was 7.

Because Melanie formed (or solidified) the belief that she might take advantage of a good person when she was 7, working with that 7-year-old, rather than with the 20-something-year-old Melanie, actually has a greater impact for cognitive awareness and change. A limiting belief is a sort of trauma. It cuts us off from the joy of life and gets frozen in our consciousness at a particular time in our development.

I'll invite Melanie to facilitate an Inquiry with her younger self as I guide her through it. You can do this on your own beliefs with a journal and two pen colors - one for you and one for your younger self - or by writing the voice of your younger self with your opposing hand.

Chana: I want you to close your eyes. Good. Now, look at Little Melanie, the 7-year-old at the table. Can you see her clearly?

Melanie: Yeah.

Chana: Ask her if you can go into the kitchen. See if you can sit down next to her.

Melanie: She's okay with that.

Chana: We're going to inquire into this belief she has, that she is taking advantage of your father. But rather than me facilitating you, *we'll facilitate her*.

Melanie: Okay.

Chana: Great. So the first question we ask is, "Is it true that you are taking advantage of Dad?"

Melanie: She's nodding.

Chana: Can you absolutely know that you're taking advantage of Dad? Can you be totally sure?

Melanie: I guess not.

Chana: How do you feel when you believe that?

Melanie: I get sad, and I'm embarrassed. I don't feel like eating.

Chana: What are you unable to do when you believe you're taking advantage of dad?

Melanie: I can't have fun with him. I can't fully enjoy dinner.

Chana: What else?

Melanie: It's hard to do my homework. It's hard to focus.

Chana: Now imagine that you're sitting there doing your homework not thinking that you're taking advantage of Dad. How are you?

Melanie: Oh. Um. Just doing my homework, which is not so hard when I can focus. And then I have time to talk to Dad about my Girl Scout troop. It's my first year and I really like it!

Chana: And how does your body feel without the thought?

Melanie: Just normal. I'm okay. My stomach isn't all knotted up.

Chana: Good. Now I'm going to ask you to play a game I call Turnaround. Okay?

Melanie: Okay.

Chana: Tell me the opposite of, "You're taking advantage of Dad."

Melanie: Um… I'm *not* taking advantage of Dad?

Chana: Yes. Great! Now, in this part of the game, we give three reasons why that's true.

Melanie: Um…

Chana: Look at his face. How do you think he feels about making dinner?

Melanie: Oh. He's happy. It looks like he likes making dinner.

Chana: Is that how you feel when you think someone is taking advantage of *you*?

Melanie: No. So, I guess I'm not taking advantage of Dad. Cool.

Chana: What's another reason?

Melanie: I didn't ask him to make dinner. He's just doing it.

Chana: What else?

Melanie: I don't know.

Chana: Big Melanie, can you help out here with an insight?

Melanie: Yeah, actually. I know about custody now; Dad didn't have to share custody, but he chose to. He wanted to be with me. And he sometimes took me home extra nights to spend even more time with me.

Chana: Which meant he'd also have to feed you.

Melanie: Yeah. He was happy to feed me. He wanted to take care of me.

Chana: So you weren't taking advantage of him.

Melanie: No.

Chana: Little Melanie, can you give me another opposite? Perhaps this time, change "him" to "me."

Melanie: I'm taking advantage of *me*?

Chana: Yes. How's that true?

Melanie: I'm not letting myself be comfortable and happy. I'm expecting myself to be all grown up. I'm not letting myself be a kid and let someone take care of me.

Chana: So even when your dad is doing something nice for you -

Melanie: I don't let it in. That sucks.

Chana: Big Melanie, are there times in your current life when you feel other are taking advantage of you?

Melanie: For sure.

Chana: Like when, for example?

Melanie: So, the last guy I went out with, Brad, he used to take advantage of me all the time.

Chana: Give me a specific example.

Melanie: One time, he asked if I wanted to rent a movie. And I said, yes. And then he asked me what movie I wanted to see. And I said, *Princess Bride*. And then he said, what about *Batman*? I said, okay. So we watched *Batman*.

Chana: How did he take advantage of you?

Melanie: We ended up seeing a movie I didn't want to see.

Chana: So why did you say that you *did* want to see it?

Melanie: I wanted him to be happy.

Chana: So who took advantage of you?

Melanie: Oh! I see! *I did*!

Chana: Yes. Why did you say you wanted to see it when you didn't?

Melanie: I didn't want him to be mad at me.

Chana: What are you afraid would happen if he was mad?

Melanie: Then he wouldn't like me anymore. He'd break up with me.

Chana: So you traded your happiness for his approval.

Melanie: That's so true.

Chana: But then you resented him for it.

Melanie: Yeah. I thought he was taking advantage of me, that he was manipulating me.

Chana: Turn it around. You were…

Melanie: I was manipulating *him*?

Chana: Manipulation is all about being sneaky and dishonest to get something from someone you don't believe they'll give you if you speak truthfully. Brad was making a suggestion of a movie he preferred. He didn't put a gun to your head, correct? Yet you lied when you said you were okay with *Batman*.

Melanie: Exactly. I wasn't honest with him. I thought he wouldn't like me if I was just myself.

Chana: Let's go back to our earlier turnaround. Give me another way you take advantage of yourself?

Melanie: Sometimes I take shifts at work even though I don't want to. I want to be super accommodating to everyone in the staff.

Chana: Everyone but you.

Melanie: Everyone but me. It means I have to cancel plans or flip my life around. It's such a pain! And then I get mad at them for asking me.

Chana: How could they be so inconsiderate!?

Melanie: (Laughs). But really, I'm not being considerate of myself.

Chana: One more way that you take advantage of yourself?

Melanie: It's not just extra shifts. I really just want to quit my job, but I feel like I'll let the team down.

Chana: So you let yourself down instead.

Melanie: Yep.

Chana: Feel that.

Melanie: I'm feeling it. This is amusing. I thought this process would hurt, but it's actually pretty funny.

Chana: Go back for a moment and picture yourself in the kitchen with your father. What do you see now?

Melanie: He's sweet. He's happy to make me dinner. He loves me and wants to do something nurturing. My dad is so great.

Chana: And how do you want to repay him for this kindness?

Melanie: I'm pretty sure he'd be happy with just a hug and, "thank you."

Chana: Can you give him that?

Melanie: Yeah. That feels good. We're both hugging dad. He's making one of his silly faces, and we're copying him and all giggling. It's a sweet moment.

Chana: So now you have a new memory.

Melanie: Yeah.

Chana: And what do you think of the idea that you were taking advantage of your father?

Melanie: That's ridiculous! He was just making me dinner. He was being Dad, and I could just be a kid.

Chana: How do you feel now?

Melanie: I want to call my dad. I want to thank him. I don't think I've thanked him enough. I've been too busy trying not to take advantage of him. But I bet that hurt him so much more.

Melanie believed a thought about herself that was discordant with her character. A trip in the **Time Machine** encouraged her to guide herself towards clarity and peace. She was not only able to feel more confident but also more grateful and loving towards her father.

> Use the **Time Machine** when you're dealing with beliefs you struggle to shake or experience as being either central to your identity yet painful and unhelpful.

There's No Business like Your Business

That which you have the power
to control, impact, and change.

There is so much we can do to render service, to make a difference in the world - no matter how large or small our circle of influence.

—Stephen R. Covey

Stephen Covey teaches a concept that has significantly impacted my family: Circles of Influence and Circles of Concern. In *The 7 Habits of Highly Effective People*, he shares that there is a slew of ideas, events, and people we get exposed to daily: the neighbors are getting a divorce, there are starving children in Africa, some politician is having an affair.

If we're exposed to these issues and are concerned about them, then they lie within our Circle of Concern.

The question is: can we *do* anything about them? Do we have the power to effect their outcomes? Are these areas where we choose to exercise the power available to us?

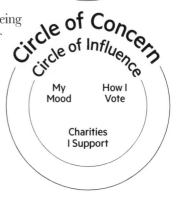

Also in my Circle of Concern is the diet I eat. Being the family chef, I exert a tremendous amount of power over which groceries I buy, what gets served at the table, and what I choose to eat. Accordingly, in addition to falling into the Circle of Concern, my diet also falls within my Circle of Influence.

The Circle of Influence includes everything in the Circle of Concern over which I have control to affect change, such as my mood, what charities I support, or how I vote in an election.

Stephen Covey says that when I focus my energy on affairs of the world that I cannot influence, my Circle of Concern expands, while my Circle of Influence shrinks, as I only have so much energy to spend.

It's also true that the more I invest in my Circle of Influence, the more it expands, and the more effective I am in the world. So, do I want to be a *concerned* citizen or an *influential* one?

When we're hanging around that part of our Circle of Concern over which we have no influence, we tend to feel angry, sad, or frustrated. Byron Katie says that's because we're mulling about in others' **Business** and have abandoned our own. We become victims of our concern about what we can't control.

Stepping into other people's **Business** can be like stepping in gum: we don't always know we've done it right away, but before long, we find ourselves stuck in one place, unable to progress forward.

We tend to think that anything we care about or that affects us is "our **Business**," but in terms of Inquiry, **Business** includes only those things over which you have immediate control and the power to affect change. In other words, your **Business** is what lies in your Circle of Influence. Let's see if Ralph's concern over his neighbor's divorce lies there as well:

> *Ralph*: They're fighting all the time, and the kids are distressed about losing their family. It's so sad because the guy is a great husband and father. He's trying so hard to be there for the kids. He didn't even want the divorce in the first place! She's being rash in leaving him.

To Ralph, this situation feels like his **Business** because these are *his* neighbors, they're in *his* community, and *he* cares about the kids and their future. The reality is that he's not the one who has to live with this marriage day in and day out. He doesn't know all the information, and he's not the one who decides to stay or go at the end of the day. He's entirely out of his **Business** and in trying to hold up his neighbors' marriage, he's divorced himself from his Circle of Influence entirely.

Chana: You believe that your neighbor shouldn't leave her husband.

Ralph: Yeah.

Chana: Can you absolutely know that it's true that she shouldn't leave him?

Ralph: Not *absolutely*.

Chana: And how do you feel when you believe the thought?

Ralph: Frustrated, angry.

Chana: What else?

Ralph: I feel lonely. Kind of abandoned. Left out.

Chana: What sensations arise in your body when you believe she shouldn't leave her husband?

Ralph: My body gets tight, I lose focus, and I want to shut down.

Chana: How do you treat yourself when you believe the thought?

Ralph: I ignore myself. My needs don't matter so much.

Chana: So you leave yourself?

Ralph: Yeah.

Chana: And how do you treat your neighbors when you believe the thought?

Ralph: I pretty much ignore the wife. So I guess I leave her too. And the husband? I pity him, the poor guy.

Chana: How do you think he feels about your pity?

Ralph: I think he gets even sadder. It's like his life is hopeless. Huh.... I didn't realize that.

Chana: So whose **Business** are you in when you believe that she shouldn't leave him?

Ralph: Mine! They're my neighbors! Our kids are friends and everything.

Chana: And how much power do you have to control their actions?

Ralph: None.

Chana: So are you in *your* **Business**?

Ralph: I'm confused.

Ralph needs to understand the concept **Business** better, so I'll guide him through the **Back in Your Business** visualization exercise. I invite you to try it as well.

Chana: Close your eyes, take some breaths, and relax. Now place your hand on the part of your body you usually do when you say, "I am." Feel the energy under your hand. Imagine all of your energy collecting into that place, and you are centered there, rather than scattered. Think, "I am, I am, I am," and feel the energy under your hand. Notice how it centers you and holds you up. Do you feel your vitality there?

Ralph: *(with his hand on his chest)* Yes. I feel calm here. Peaceful. My mind is quiet. It's like sitting on a warm sofa.

Ralph's focus and energy are coming back into himself, back into his own **Business**.

Chana: Now, imagine your neighbor standing in front of his house, and you are believing the thought that his wife shouldn't leave him. Feel what happens to that energy under your hand. Does it change in any way? Does it stay where it is or go elsewhere?

Ralph: It's all shaky and agitated. And it's not in me anymore. I see it over in the distance - with him.

Chana: Is it *really* with him, or does it just hover?

Ralph: It's hovering.

Chana: How much power do you have over there?

Ralph: None. I can't change his situation no matter how much I think about trying to.

Chana: And now that the energy has left you, what do you feel in your body?

Ralph: It feels empty. Sad. My body wants to collapse.

Chana: This is because you've left yourself, your **Business**, your power center, and you hopped over into your neighbor's **Business**.

Ralph: Oh. I get it. Even though he's my neighbor, I can't change him, and for sure can't change his wife.

Chana: Now, take a deep breath and imagine yourself back at your neighbor's house without the thought that she shouldn't leave him. How are you without it?

Ralph: I'm more relaxed and more present. Like when I put my hand on my chest.

Chana: So, let's turn it around. What's the opposite of she shouldn't leave him?

Ralph: She *should* leave him?

Chana: Yes. Give me three reasons why that's true.

Ralph: She doesn't look too happy.

Chana: Did you pay attention to that when you believed she *shouldn't*?

Ralph: No. It wasn't relevant at all.

Chana: That's good to notice. Give me two more reasons she should leave him.

Ralph: They fight *all the time*. We can even hear it from my bedroom at night. They tried counseling, and it was a total flop.

Chana: And another one?

Ralph: Actually, one of their kids told my daughter that she's so sick of all the fighting. The kids might rather their parents didn't live together.

Chana: Now let's turn it around again. Put yourself in the picture this time.

Ralph: I shouldn't leave him.

Chana: How's that true?

Ralph: When I'm busy pitying him, I can't really be his friend. It's like I'm looking down at him. Also, I'm not helping him believe he has the strength to survive this. People get divorced all the time and move on, but it must be hard for him when his friend is pushing him to fight reality all the time.

Chana: And what else?

Ralph: He could use support right now. I could spend more time with him. We could go out for a beer once a week; I bet he'd love that. And it wouldn't be as heavy as complaining in his backyard, which is usually where we end up when we do hang out. I thought that to be a good friend I had to put down his wife and resent her, but he might need some fun in his life instead.

Chana: And you?

Ralph: Totally. I don't want to be in such a negative place either.

Chana: What's another turnaround, perhaps this time about *your marriage*? We want to focus on *your* **Business**.

Ralph: I shouldn't leave…. my wife.

Chana: Tell me about that.

Ralph: When I'm busy thinking about them, I'm not present for her. There are so many ways I could be a better husband.

Chana: That's where your power is. In your choices, your behaviors. So how can you be more present for your wife?

Ralph: She loves massages. I can offer them more than I do. And when we got married, I said I would do the dishes, but mostly she does them. I could do more stuff like that around the house.

Chana: And one more?

Ralph: I haven't surprised her with anything romantic in …. Wow…. In a *long* time. I should take her swing dancing. We both enjoy that.

Chana: How does it feel to be in your **Business**?

Ralph: Empowering. These are things I can *do*. I got so caught up in my neighbors' lives, I didn't even realize I wasn't showing up in my own.

Chana: Now I'm going to push you to come up with one more turnaround. You shouldn't leave…

Ralph: Myself?

Chana: Yes. When you are busy in your neighbor's **Business**, who's with *you*?

Ralph: Oh. I leave myself. I feel incredibly lonely then.

Chana: So give me three reasons why you shouldn't leave yourself is true.

Ralph: I shouldn't leave myself because I need my energy for all the things I want to do in my life. And … because I hate the way it feels.

Chana: What else?

Ralph: Because then I'm in my **Business**.

Chana: Yes.

Ralph: That's where I want to be.

It's easy to wallow in our Circle of Concern and judge others' behavior. It's also completely disheartening. Although focusing on our own actions requires a lot more work, it's far more effective and empowering. The more we take the judgments we have of others and point them back to ourselves, the more we can learn about how to create meaningful change for the better. With every empowered action we take, we increase our Circle of Influence.

Use the **Back in Your Business** visualization to when you want to come back to your center and find ease. By understanding what being in your **Business** feels like, you're more empowered to live from that place and learn that there's **No Business Like Your Business**!

Download a **No Business Like Your Business** worksheet from the **Free Bonus Section** of my website:

Hold.ChanaMason.com/bonus.

The Courtroom

The place our minds go to in an attempt to "objectively" judge ourselves and our experiences.

> *What we can or cannot do, what we consider possible or impossible, is rarely a function of our true capability. It is more likely a function of our beliefs about who we are.*
>
> —Tony Robbins

H eather came to me looking for some direction in life, but every time we tried engaging in a visualization process to imagine what a compelling future would look like, she'd derail the conversation. I finally confronted her about it:

Chana: What is so challenging for you about imagining an exciting future for yourself?

Heather: It's hard to believe any of that stuff can actually happen.

Chana: Why?

Heather: Because I couldn't do all the work required to make it happen.

Chana: Why do you believe that?

Heather: I'm lazy. I've always been lazy. I don't ever follow through on stuff.

Chana: So let's take a look at that belief. Perhaps it's worth questioning.

Heather: Okay.

Chana: Can you think of a time you firmly believed you're lazy?

Heather: Yes. Last week when I was sitting in front of the computer. I was supposed to be working on a resume to apply for jobs. But I was checking Instagram instead.

Chana: You're lazy. Is it true?

Heather: Yeah. I'm wasting time.

Chana: Can you absolutely know that you're lazy?

Heather: Of course.

Chana: How do you react when you believe that you're lazy?

Heather: My body sags. I feel drained.

Chana: What else?

Heather: I want to curl up into a ball and hide under the covers. I feel depressed.

Chana: What are you afraid would happen if you didn't believe you're lazy?

Heather: Then I would never get *anything* done. My apartment would be disgusting!

Chana: And tell me, what are you not able to do when you believe the thought?

Heather: I don't want to do anything except curl up in bed with a bag of chips.

Chana: So is the thought helping you get stuff done?

Heather: No. Not at all. Gosh. Just the opposite.

Chana: That's usually how it goes. And whose **Business** are you in when you believe the thought?

Heather: Mine. I'm talking about myself, right?

The most insidious way we leave our **Business** is when we judge ourselves with statements such as:

I should lose weight

I'm not smart enough

I deserve better

I'm selfish

We think we're in our **Business** because we believe our thoughts *are* us. What we miss is that, in believing these judgments, we leave our center of power entirely. To help Heather understand this, I guided her through the **Back in Your Business** visualization.

Chana: Close your eyes. Breathe deeply and place your hand where you usually do when you say, "I am." Feel the energy under your hand. This is your power center; it's where you hold the energy that vitalizes you, holds up your body, and drives your actions. Now, think of another person in your life who you often define as lazy. Got it?

Heather: Yes. This guy Greg from work.

Chana: Now I want you to feel what happens to that energy under your hand when you believe the thought, "He's lazy."

Heather: It just floods out of me. Just seeps out of my toes and goes oozing over to Greg.

Chana: And what happens to your body?

Heather: It collapses. Like a puppet.

Chana: Nothing is holding you up anymore?

Heather: Yes. And I feel sad. And angry here.

Chana: Because you've left yourself. You've left your **Business**.

Heather: I can feel that.

Chana: And you're over there in Greg's **Business**.

Heather: But not really. I can't change him or anything.

Chana: Exactly. It's just wishful thinking except for the part about your loss of energy.

Heather: Yes. That feels very real.

Chana: Because it is. Now shake it up and clear the air. Take another deep breath and feel your energy again. Good. Now, notice what happens when you believe that *you're* lazy.

Heather: Uch. Yuck. Same thing. I'm drained.

Chana: You've left your **Business**.

Heather: But where could I go? This isn't about Greg; it's about *me*.

Chana: You've left yourself to jump into **The Courtroom**. You're not only playing the prosecuting attorney, claiming that you're lazy. You're also in the judge's seat and the jury box deciding the verdict!

Heather: Why?

Chana: Because to judge something, we have to stand outside of it and, clipboard in hand, make all sorts of assessments about it. We leave ourselves in order to judge ourselves.

Heather: Ok. I get it. I'm no longer present in the moment. It's like I'm watching myself.

Chana: Exactly.

We score ourselves against a Platonic standard of what is an ideal amount of intelligence or beauty or strength, not just for ourselves, but for the situation. This judgement requires a level of knowledge that's beyond human. It's pure arrogance to think we can know such things. When Heather describes herself as lazy, she assumes she knows precisely how much effort the universe is demanding of her at any given moment and of how much she's capable. She's simply invented the standard to which she compares himself. It's not real. Every human's capacity is unique, so there is no accurate metric.

Chana: Now, the question is: According to what standard are you assessing yourself?

Heather: I never thought about that. Well, in school, they told us how much homework we were supposed to do and how hard we had to work to get an A. So I guess that?

Chana: Did every teacher have the same standards?

Heather: No.

Chana: So whose standard did you bring into **The Courtroom**?

Heather: That's a good question. I guess my dad's. He's crazy industrious. And my favorite teacher in high school. My biology teacher, Mr. Adams. He gave us a test every Monday, and I loved doing well on them. I usually made the curve. The other kids made fun of me and threw spitballs at me because they wanted the curve to be lower. But inside, I was so proud of myself.

Chana: And who decided to put those standards into **The Courtroom**?

Heather: Oh! Me!

Chana: So whose standards are they?

Heather: Mine.

Chana: Can you absolutely know you are capable of meeting those standards at all times and in all circumstances?

Heather: No. I can't.

Chana: And can you know whether that standard of work is exactly what you or the universe needs?

Heather: No. Not at all.

Chana: How does the standard of industriousness that you've created make you feel?

Heather: Horrible. It's so much pressure; I can't think straight. I want to run away.

Chana: So it makes you less industrious.

Heather: Exactly. That's so sad.

Chana: Can you think of a peaceful reason to keep this standard?

Heather: No. It's stressful.

Chana: Let's try turning the thought around. In dealing with these type of beliefs, we benefit greatly from switching the subject of the statement from "I" to "my thinking."

Heather: My thinking is lazy.

Chana: Yes. Give me three reasons that's true.

Heather: My thinking doesn't work to show me all the ways that I've pushed myself to achieve my goals. My thinking focuses on the same tiny collection of thoughts all day. It's such a waste of time, and it's exhausting.

Chana: Good. One more.

Heather: It's busy judging me, rather than trying to find solutions to problems. And my thinking wastes a lot of time whining over things I can't change.

Chana: It pushes you into **The Courtroom**.

Heather: Which is a fantasy. It would be much more useful to complete the task in front of me. Like my resume. Without the thought, it actually feels like a much smaller task.

Helping ourselves feel empowered to effect real change in our lives is the most powerful thing we can do as facilitators of our growth. Coming back into our **Business** and focusing on staying there is a key tool for inspiring that empowerment.

Use **The Courtroom** image to better understand how, in judging yourself, you've left your **Business**. By trying to attain some ultimate ideal for your life, you lead yourself down a path to suffering.

The Addiction Loop and Aggression Tailspin

Patterns of destructive thought and behavior that repeatedly fuel each other.

All action results from thought,
so it is thoughts that matter.

—*Sai Baba*

D o you ever leave the news running in the background because you "need to keep your thumb on the pulse of what's happening?" or eat just one more bite of the chocolate cake even though your stomach is about to burst?

Perhaps someone cuts you off on the highway, and you blow your top or your favorite piece of china breaks, and you kick the wall in a fury, stubbing your toe in the process.

In this chapter, we're going to dig into the spinning wheels of **Addiction and Aggression**. When I say **Addiction**, I don't just mean drugs or alcohol. I'm talking about the array of behaviors we ALL do to escape, like unhealthy eating, binging on social media, or working long hours. Similarly, **Aggression** is any mood that takes over your entire being and leaves you and others wallowing in regret.

Most of us take comfort in the fact that our **Addictions and Aggressions** are socially acceptable enough that no one pushes us to jump into rehab, but these behaviors wreak havoc on our lives every day, and not just because they keep us from living healthy lifestyles. It's because they keep us from facing one of our greatest teachers: pain.

You may be thinking: Pain - A teacher? How could that be? Karla learned exactly how after a session that began with her calling me in a huff.

Chana: What's wrong?

Karla: I've been working on a blog post for hours. I spent the past few days on it, and yesterday my computer crashed and erased the whole thing!

Notice that Karla has simply stated a collection of facts: She *was* working, and the computer *did* crash. But our brain doesn't just process facts; it colors the experience through the lens of our beliefs, which is why Karla's voice is charged with frustration.

Chana: And why are you upset?

Karla: What do you mean? Of course I'm upset! Wouldn't you be upset if your work was erased?

Chana: If I were upset, I would have my reasons. What is more important here are what *your* reasons are. What does it mean to you that your work got erased? (**ATM**)

Karla: I… I don't know.

Chana: Take a moment to breathe and think about it. Your computer crashed, and your blog post was erased. And that means…

Karla: It means that, as usual, things just don't work out for me.

Bingo! Here's why Karla's frustrated. It's not the computer crash, but rather the *grand symbolism* of it.

Chana: How do you react when you believe that things don't work out for you?

Karla: Ugh. My body sinks. I feel weak.

Chana: Any emotions come up?

Karla: Yeah… I feel sad. And frustrated. I want to give up.

Chana: What are you unable to do when you believe that things don't work out for you?

Karla: I can't remember what I wrote. I can't sit at the computer and try again. And… Oh yeah… I don't even think of asking one of my computer savvy friends to try and help me recover the file. It just feels hopeless.

Chana: Any movies playing in your mind?

Karla: Yes. Of all the times that things went bust. My middle school science project… Now I see the big fat F at the top of my college history paper and the nasty haircut I got when I was 8. It's such a miserable movie. That's why I couldn't sleep last night. It was the "Karla's a Loser" rerun special.

Any motivation to move forward has drained out of Karla. In a nutshell, she's in mental and physical pain. For most of us, pain is tremendously uncomfortable.

Our culture pushes us to avoid it at all costs. So what do we do to combat it? We muster up our two best friends: fight and flight.

Fight manifests as rebellion, anger, and blame. In other words, **Aggression**:

Chana: What did you do while you couldn't sleep?

Karla: This is so embarrassing. I recorded a very obnoxious message to my friend Allison. She's the one who encouraged me to start the blog in the first place. I fumed at her for like five minutes. I'm so humiliated.

Chana: Why?

Karla: Because now she probably hates me.

The **Aggression Tailspin** has begun. Karla's believing a thought that causes her pain, and to fight it, she's gets aggressive, but the aggression leads her either back to her original belief or a similarly destructive one.

Chana: And how do you react when you believe that she probably hates you?

Karla: Believe it or not, this morning, when I looked in the mirror, I actually slapped myself.

Chana: You didn't like the upset you experienced when you believed that nothing works out for you, so you tried to get it out on Allison.

Karla: Yeah.

Chana: But what did that lead to?

Karla: More pain. Oh… and more aggression. I could be running in this loop forever if I don't stop.

Flight seems more demure than fight, because we're just running away. Flight manifests itself as **Addiction**, which includes screen time and drugs, but also behaviors we often label as "psychotic," like dark or obsessive thinking. Hard though it may be to believe, thoughts of self-harm are an addiction that allows us to escape the excruciating story we might be telling ourselves about our lives. It can keep us so busy that we don't have to face our rotting pile of pain.

Karla's sleepless night has me wondering whether this situation is an addiction trigger. Only one way to find out:

Chana: Did any addictions come up for you when you believed that things don't work out for you?

Karla: Yeah. Last night, after my hideous message to Allison, I went straight for my favorite comforts: chocolate chunk ice cream and a trashy novel. I know it's bad for me and so fattening, but last night, I didn't care.

We already see that Karla judges her addictive behavior as bad, fattening, and trashy, and I'm guessing there's more judgment on the way:

Chana: How do you feel about the ice cream and novel now?

Karla: Lousy. It just further proves that nothing ever works out for me.

Chana: Why?

Karla: Because for one, I broke my resolution to stop eating sweets; two, I didn't keep my commitment to finish my blog on time; and three, I wasted hours doing *nothing*.

Karla has added three new neural pathways to this belief, so it's become stronger inside her brain. On top of that, renewing it makes her feel even worse. She now has a heftier mound of pain to face.

Chana: Karla, when you believe all that, what do you want to do?

Karla: Honestly? This is going to sound ridiculous, but… I want more ice cream.

Exactly! And I'm sure as she opens the freezer she'll be telling herself, "This'll be the very last one…" Then she'll feel yuckier, which will lead to more ice cream and, of course, more yuck. Karla would become a hamster in a cage, stuck running 'round and 'round in the **Addiction Loop**.

A person can easily spin in and between both the **Aggression Tailspin** and the **Addiction Loop**, jumping from anger to cocaine to violence to pizza. That's why we see rage and addiction packaged together in so many people.

We may crazy-eight in and out of the **Addiction Loop** and **Aggression Tailspin**, so it's important to see them as a paired system. The diagram below shows you how seemingly out-of-control behavior has a logical progression and an available remedy:

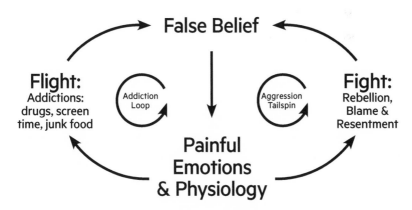

How do we stop these crazy cycles? By activating courage. Brene Brown teaches that courage is the strength to share what's in our heart, to be vulnerable with our emotions. I believe that since we are our own worst critics, we're also our most challenging audience and the one we have to open up to the most.

First, Karla has to allow herself to feel the sadness that's sinking her body and motivation to the ground.

Karla: It's so uncomfortable. I wish I could just have the ice cream.

Chana: Do you *really* want the ice cream?

Karla: No. I'd rather have peace and a good night's rest.

Chana: So close your eyes and go back to the moment when you realized that your file was erased. Breathe and permit yourself to *feel* without judging the feelings or wishing them away.

Karla: Okay, I'm in it.

Chana: The file was deleted, and you're upset, but are you okay?

Karla: Huh. I never thought of it that way. Yeah, I'm okay. I'm not dying or anything.

Chana: The question is, do you want to continue to feel how you're feeling?

Karla: For sure not!

Chana: So what do you need to do?

Karla: Um… ask, "What's the thought?" It's the one I mentioned earlier. Nothing ever works out for me.

Karla's pain is a guide: the physical suffering created by her thoughts is her body's way of letting her know that she's somehow fighting reality. If she doesn't want to keep suffering, she'll need to reassess her thinking.

Chana: Is it true that things don't ever work out for you?

Karla: Feels like it.

Chana: Can you absolutely know that it's true that things don't ever work out for you?

Karla: No.

Chana: We have a pretty good idea of how you react when you believe the thought. I'd like you to take a moment to imagine yourself in front of the computer *without* believing that things don't ever work out for you?

Karla: I'm annoyed that I lost my file, but I don't feel devastated. My body isn't sinking to the ground. I'm in more of a problem-solving mode.

Chana: Do you have any cravings for ice cream without the thought?

Karla: No, I simply want to get the blog done. I can see myself calling a friend to try and retrieve the file or just starting over again. I'll finish later than I hoped, but the rewrite will be much faster because I have my thoughts organized better now than when I first started.

Chana: Great. Open your eyes again and give me a turnaround for, "Things don't ever work out for me."

Karla: Things *do* work out for me.

Chana: Give me three reasons why that's as true or truer than your original thought.

Karla: Even though my computer crashed, it's up and working again. I'm excited about the ideas in this post and know that even though it'll take me extra hours of work, it's going to be a good one.

Chana: One more.

Karla: My blog has been getting more popular every week. It's working out for me, even though I was originally hesitant to start sharing my ideas on the Internet.

Chana: Wow. That's inspiring. Can you give me another turnaround?

Karla: *My thinking* doesn't ever work out for me.

Chana: And that's true because...?

Karla: I had this minor setback, and my thinking turned it into a major saga. People lose files all the time. It doesn't have to *mean* anything other than that it would be a good idea for me to back up my files.

Chana: Why else is it true?

Karla: My thinking was focused on judging me and my life rather than on solving the challenge I had in front of me. And it led me to binge on ice cream... which I think I'm never buying again. If it's not there, I'll be more likely to do Inquiry next time.

Chana: Sounds like a courageous move.

Karla. Yeah. Thanks!

Escaping pain might feel good in the short run, but deprives us of the opportunity to learn and grow beyond the limiting beliefs that pin us down into feeling small and behaving in ways that cause us further suffering. Identifying **Aggression** and **Addiction**, stopping them in their tracks, and questioning the beliefs that get us there is the boldest exit from the roller coaster.

> Identify **The Addiction Loop and Aggression Tailspin** when you're consistently using your "drugs" of choice or engaging in harmful behavior to avoid the pain caused by unexamined beliefs. Take the courage to face your pain and identify the false beliefs fueling it. You can then do Inquiry and move towards peace, joy, and light.

A Fresh Pair of Lenses:
UPENDING YOUR SUFFERING

*It's often been said that "seeing is believing",
but in many cases, the reverse is also true.
Believing results in seeing.*

—Donald L. Hicks

When you shift your consciousness, you see reality with a whole different light. If you are aligned with truth, that light shines a whole lot brighter, but it can also be glaringly bright. How? You'll have to face all the places that your false beliefs have led you to behave in ways that are dishonest, inconsiderate, sneaky, or downright mean. That can hurt. At the same time, facing your demons and taking responsibility for them, can be the most liberating, honorable, and esteem-building act you'll ever take. In this section, we'll dig into how you can shift your perspective, act on new understandings, and build a life in alignment with your highest self.

The Little Green Troll

A mischievous creature who voices
your negative thoughts and has
a weakness for Snickers.

The next time you have a thought... let it go.

—*Ron White*

Samantha felt as though she was going insane because her sleep was often interrupted by her toddler, Alex. Multiple times a night, he'd hobble into her room and cry for attention. He wanted water, needed to go to the bathroom, was scared, wanted milk, or who knows what else! She woke up exhausted and cranky every morning — so did Alex.

Chana: What, for you, is the most upsetting part of the situation?

Sam: That he keeps coming into my room. He should be sleeping through the night already.

Chana: Does it bother you more that he's coming into your room or that he's not sleeping through the night?

Sam: What's bothering me most is that he's waking me up. I want to be able to sleep!

Chana: So you believe he shouldn't wake you up.

Sam: Yes! He's almost two already. It's enough!

Chana: Can you absolutely know that it's true that he shouldn't wake you up?

Sam: Yes.

Chana: How do you react when you believe that?

Sam: Angry. This sounds horrible, but I want to yell at him and hurt him. I have to hold myself back from that. And then I feel guilty for being such a bad mom.

Chana: What sensations arise in your body when you believe he shouldn't wake you up?

Sam: My chest gets hot and tight. Everything gets tense. I'm so mad; so annoyed.

Chana: What are you unable to do when you believe the thought?

Sam: I can't think straight. I can't be calm.

Chana: Can you think of a peaceful reason to keep the thought?

Sam: It helps me to focus on getting him back to bed.

Chana: Is that peaceful?

Sam: No. I'm grouchy the whole time.

Chana: So, can you think of a peaceful reason to keep the thought that he shouldn't wake you up?

Sam: Oh. No.

Chana: Now. Close your eyes and take a slow, deep breath. Imagine you're lying in bed and your son has just come into your room. How would you be without the thought that he shouldn't wake you up?

Sam: I don't even know how to answer that question. He's there. I'm just so pissed.

Chana: Can you move the thought to the side for a minute? How does your son look without the thought?

Sam: How could the thought not *be* there? It's so *there*.

Sam found it challenging to imagine her life without the thought, and she's not alone; it can often be the most challenging part of Inquiry. In that situation, I find using an imagery tool helps, especially one of Sam's creation.

Chana: Okay. I want you to imagine that this thought is being said by some sort of creature who's in the room with you. What do you see?

Sam: A **Little Troll**. He's pea green and hairy with big ears.

Chana: Great. Picture him as clearly as you can. What does he smell like?

Sam: He smells like rotten sewage. Gross.

Chana: What does his voice sound like? Is it really vivid?

Sam: Yes. High pitched and nasal. No way I can sleep with him around.

Chana: Ask him what his favorite food is.

Sam: He loves Snickers.

Chana: Perfect. Can you give him $100 and send him off to the convenience store? Tell him he can buy as many Snickers bars as he wants. He can buy out the store if he wants to!

Sam: He's so excited, he's squealing!

Sam's so identified with the belief that it's difficult for her to imagine it not being there. Some people are challenged to imagine themselves without a thought because they fear it requires them to create a vacuum in their minds, which feels uncomfortable. By forming the **Little Green Troll**, Sam literally "sees" the thought leaving her without the anxiety of detachment or the need to fill the space with something else. Remember, this personified being can be anything from a rabbit to a hobbit, but the **Troll** imagery worked for Sam. Who likes having a **Troll** around?

Chana: Send the **Troll** off now and watch him leave with his $100. Now it's just you and your son in the room. How are you without the **Troll** there?

Sam: I can see my son. He's so cute and is struggling to stay asleep. I'm more relaxed and can be more sympathetic to him.

Chana: Now let's see what this thought is here to teach you. Turn it around. What's the 180 degree opposite of, "He shouldn't wake you up?"

Sam: He *should* wake me up.

Chana: Give me three reasons it's true.

Sam: He depends on me for everything, and he's used to asking me for help when he needs it. Nighttime can be lonely and scary, and he doesn't feel capable of getting to bed on his own.

Chana: Good. Can you give me another turnaround?

Sam: *I* shouldn't wake me up.

Chana: How is that true?

Sam: Oooh. So many times I say I'm going to get to bed by ten, but then I'll stay up reading articles on my phone until midnight.

Chana: So you're keeping yourself up.

Sam: Yeah. Even when Alex has nothing to do with it.

Chana: What's another reason you shouldn't wake yourself up?

Sam: Because I need rest. Because I want to have a full night of sleep.

Chana: What else?

Sam: I don't know.

Chana: Think specifically about this situation with Alex. How are you waking yourself up?

Sam: Duh!

Chana: Why did you say that?

Sam: I just realized that his waking up has something to do with me. He never learned to stay in bed because *I* never taught him how! I never thought of it that way.

Chana: What way?

Sam: I never taught Alex to go to sleep on his own. I've always held him or rocked him or nursed him. He's doesn't know how to fall asleep, so if he wakes up, he comes to me.

Chana: Yes.

Sam: By not teaching him, I've set him up to wake me up. I'm doing it. I'm waking me up!

Chana: That's a very different perspective.

Sam: Very. If I want to sleep through the night, I have to teach Alex to.

Chana: Or you could choose that it's more important to you that Alex not have to go to sleep alone.

Sam: I could choose that. But at least now I know I have a choice. I know what I can do.

Chana: You're back in your **Business**.

Sam: Yeah. That feels good.

By imagining her belief to be the cackle of a **Little Green Troll**, Sam was not only able to disassociate herself from it, but also to lighten her reaction to it. I've heard other practitioners say they offer other imagery tools to their clients to help put a thought on hold. It can be sprayed out with window cleaner, blasted up in a rocket ship, shoved in a drawer, buried into the ground, or written on a piece of paper and crunched in your hand. I find personification not only useful but playful and fun; **The Little Green Troll** isn't so bad when he's gorging on Snickers.

Use **The Little Green Troll** when you're having a difficult time imagining yourself living without a thought that's causing your suffering. Putting the thought into the mouth of a creature helps you imagine your life without it.

Lessons from Your Opponent

An understanding that the thoughts that
bring you suffering will also teach you
your most important life lessons.

A subtle thought that is in error may
yet give rise to fruitful inquiry that
can establish truths of great value.

—Isaac Asimov

G reat philosophers, religious leaders, and mystics speak of the freedom, peace, and serenity that come from a detached and joyful plane of consciousness. Some say we gain serenity by simply brushing thoughts aside. Inquiry doesn't treat a stressful belief as an opponent we have to evade or subdue; instead, we invite the thought to fully inhabit our space for a while and invite it to teach us its lessons. Just like every circumstance and person we encounter offers us the opportunity to learn and grow, thoughts themselves can be our greatest teachers. Inquiry trains us to become active, questioning observers of our thinking, rather than its passive victims.

Linda struggled with depression and floated in and out of therapists' offices, never finding the relief she was seeking. Most sessions with clinicians left her feeling worse than when she walked in. She was curious to see if Inquiry might lead her in a different direction. The first thing she wanted to work on was her relationship with her mother:

Linda: I just can't get over it.

Chana: What can't you get over?

Linda: That Mom doesn't love me.

Chana: You mom doesn't love you: Is that true?

Linda: Yes.

Chana: Can you absolutely know that it's true?

Linda: It's obvious.

Chana: And how do you react when you believe that she doesn't love you?

Linda: I want to ball myself up in the darkest corner of my basement and disappear. I don't want to talk to anyone.

The Anatomy of Feedback shows us that if a thought makes us shut down, we can *know* that it's *not* true. That being said, your brain will continue to ignore facts or twist reality to fit your bias until you explore other ways of believing. That's when your mind will shift its perception and reveal everything you didn't see before; in other words, you'll have an "Aha!" moment.

The lessons of a thought lie in its opposites, what Byron Katie calls *turnarounds*. A thought is like a many-sided crystal: in every direction, refractions of light reveal glimmers of truth flipped upside down from what we initially believed them to be. Linda's emotions are delicate. She's sunk into a dark place, and it's neither necessary or healthy for her to hang out there too long. Let's jump right to the turnarounds:

Chana: What is the opposite of the thought that your mother doesn't love you?

Linda: To fully learn from a turnaround, you have to give your mind the space to find proofs and let them rise to the surface. See what comes up when I ask you: how is this new thought as true or truer than the original?

Linda: Um… I guess she didn't throw me into a dumpster.

Chana: Good. What else?

Linda: She bought me clothes, wiped my butt, fed me.

Chana: And…

Linda: Umm… She buys me birthday presents.

Just like a stool needs at least three legs to stand, you need at least three solid reasons that support a new thought. If you're trying to upend a particularly insidious belief, I recommend you search for even more. In looking for proofs, be creative, allow yourself to use figurative language, and most importantly, be honest.

Chana: Stop for a minute and think of a time she gave you a birthday present. Notice what you have to do to believe she doesn't love you while she's handing it to you.

Linda: Ooof. It's pretty bad. I don't even allow eye contact. I'm thinking of how she's trying to buy my affection and manipulate me.

Chana: She couldn't possibly be loving you with the gift, could she?

Linda: No. I probably don't even thank her.

Chana: Cut the "probably."

Linda: Right. I don't thank her. Man, that feels so crappy.

Chana: What do you want to do?

Linda: I should thank her. I don't know if I've ever thanked her for much of anything…

Linda recognized that for her depression to lift, she needed to become an active participant in her life, rather than a victim of circumstance. The first step Linda took was to write a letter of gratitude to her mother for everything she'd done for her. She scheduled that important step into her calendar for later that evening.

The thought *my mother doesn't love me* holds many lessons that can be revealed by stating its opposite. Turning thoughts around can happen by flipping the subject, object, or verb of any given statement. In Linda's case, she came up with:

1. My mother does love me.	Negate the verb
2. My mother doesn't hate me.	Say the opposite of the verb
3. My mother doesn't love herself.	Say the opposite of the object
4. I don't love me.	Say the opposite of the subject
5. My thinking doesn't love me.	Replace the subject with my thinking (i.e. The seat of all the thoughts that come my way)
6. I don't love my mother.	Say the opposite of the subject and object (and possibly the verb)
7. My mother doesn't love me, and that's okay.	Add and that's okay to the original statement

Not all opposite statements resonate as logical or true. See how a new thought feels in your body. Be aware that an intense, discomforting, or knee-jerk reaction can often indicate a turnaround has powerful lessons to teach you that require you to take responsibility or face an ugly truth about yourself (which can be excruciating sometimes.)

Turnaround #5 above is important to clarify because the concept of separating our essence from our "thinking" is not immediately apparent. Our thinking is there to serve us, but when it feeds us such thoughts as: "My mother doesn't love me," "I'm a loser," or "I'll never make anything of my life," then it's working completely against us. We want to remind ourselves that our thinking should be under our control, not the other way around. When Linda alters, "I don't love me" to, "My thinking doesn't love me," she can recognize just how cruelly her thinking is treating her.

Turnarounds can also be metaphorical. In the chapter **Should-ing Belongs in the Outhouse**, Sandy realized that she, like the terrorists in Jerusalem, was "stabbing" other people by behaving distrustfully towards her friends and imagining stabbings hundreds of times in her mind. Her believing that "People shouldn't stab other people" only served to make her as angry and violent while she was seeking world peace.

As you become more experienced with turnarounds, you'll learn that they don't always have to be a perfect opposite of the original statement. Turnaround #7 above is a perfect example. Adding, "and that's okay" doesn't reverse an original statement; rather, it invalidates the *implication* that the believer is incapable of accepting its truth.

Chana: Give me three reasons it's true that your mother doesn't love you and that's okay?

Linda: Well, I've lived for 32 years believing she didn't love me and I've survived.

Chana: What else?

Linda: She likes buying stuff, so she gives me gifts. I'd prefer we spend quality time together, but she's still loves me in her own way, and even if I don't feel the love, receiving the gifts is better than rejecting them entirely. I feel better.

Chana: Can you give me one more reason that your mother doesn't love you and that's okay?

Linda: Um.... I... I'm trying hard here, but I just... I can't *really* believe that. It can't be okay.

172

Linda's stuck. She doesn't want to live in a reality in which her mother doesn't love her. A trip to the **ATM** can help us uncover her reasons why:

Chana: I want you to complete this sentence: your mother doesn't love you **and that means**...

Linda: It means there's something wrong with me. That I'm unlovable.

Chana: Anything else?

Linda: That I can't move on. The world would come crashing down around me.

Chana: And...

Linda: I wouldn't be worthy. Ugh, this is so screwed up!

Chana: What's screwed up?

Linda: This whole thing. It's like her love is what holds up my entire existence.

Chana: Do you really believe that?

Linda: Well... what did you just ask?

Chana: What do you remember?

Linda: Something about me believing that her love holds me up.

Chana: Do you believe it?

Linda: Oh. Huh. Wait... that would mean that only people whose moms loved them would stay alive. But that's not true. My friend Janet loved her son to pieces, but he still died of cancer. And there are moms too drugged up to even recognize their kids, and plenty of those kids still survive.

Chana: So what does that mean?

Linda: I guess that something's holding up my existence that has nothing to do with Mom.

Chana: How do you feel?

Linda: Pretty good, actually. Cause here I am, and I saw before that

Mom does love me in all sorts of ways. Even when she doesn't, I keep existing. It's nice if she loves me, but I can be okay without it.

Chana: What does that mean?

Linda: It feels less desperate. I get it now: she could *not* love me, and it would be okay. I bet there are times that I drive her nuts with my theater obsession or crazy boyfriends and she doesn't feel so loving then. And I'm okay. If I'm honest with myself, the world doesn't come crashing down.

Chana: And what about your mom?

Linda: She's doing her thing, and I'm doing mine.

Chana: How do you feel?

Linda: Good, actually. I don't *need* her to love me, but I can choose to take in the love that she does give me. I like that. I feel warm inside.

Linda might have wanted to erase the thought that her mother doesn't love her and live in the place of no-thought, but it wouldn't have been realistic for her to do so. Aristotle said, "Nature abhors a vacuum," and the human mind is quite similar. For Linda to live without her original belief, she first needed to learn from it by replacing it with others that would build her compassion, self-acceptance, and happiness.

Rooted in Linda's discomfort was the belief that she *needed* her mother's love. This neediness caused her to panic because, subconsciously, she was aware of the fact that human affection is not static and that her mother wouldn't live forever. The greatest **Lesson From Her Opponent** - *my mother doesn't love me* - was the realization that she was just fine *with or without* her mother's love. She freed herself to enjoy whatever love came her way.

Glean **Lessons From Your Opponent** when you want break the painful shackles created by untrue thinking. The opposites of the beliefs causing your distress will teach you how to live in integrity with your values.

Action Superhero

A person who lives out the understanding that
our thinking is cemented by our actions as much
as our actions are the results of beliefs.

Do you want to know who you are? Don't ask!
Actions will delineate and define you.

—Thomas Jefferson

Our beliefs are the products of neural networks strengthened through repetition, evidence, and reinforcing behavior. Let's say toddler Johnny, while learning to walk, hears, "How clumsy" every time he falls over. That repetition may ingrain the belief that he's clumsy, and he'll interpret each misstep going forward through that lens and use it as further evidence of his clumsiness. Through the years, the neural connections around the belief become thicker and stronger, further encouraging him to leap to "I'm clumsy" whenever he's looking to understand a situation in which his body doesn't function perfectly.

What fully cements the belief in Johnny's mind is **Action**. Perhaps he won't try out for soccer when he's nice, or he'll hesitate to learn how to cook because he's scared to handle dangerous utensils in the kitchen. He wants to believe his behavior is justified, so he'll further reinforce the idea that he's clumsy with other supporting thoughts like "I'm not coordinated," "I've never been good at sports," or "Cooking is not my thing." **Action** has the dual effect of strengthening the original neural connections and building a web of beliefs around them, a veritable **Tower of Babble**.

Offering at least three pieces of evidence holding up a turnaround strengthens a new neural pathway, and the more we support this alternative perspective, the more ingrained it will become. After we've completed an Inquiry, we can search daily for more evidence. Johnny can reinforce the turnaround, "I'm not clumsy," by noting all the things he does effectively each day, like drive his car to work, eat without spilling his food, and fold his clothes into neat piles. He can also take **Action** by trying out for sports and cooking dinner. Johnny can also create a **Tower of Benefit** to support his new understanding with thoughts such as, "Sports involve a lot of trial and error," "No one gets the ball in the goal every time."

In **Lessons From Your Opponent**, Linda was dealing with the belief that her mother didn't love her. Her fourth turnaround, "I don't love me," proved particularly insightful.

Chana: Can you tell me some ways you haven't been very loving towards yourself?

Linda: Well… I *love* bubble baths, but I take one maybe once a year. I'm often exhausted by 10pm but will keep myself up another hour folding laundry or something. And… I never wear the jewelry Mom's given me. It's shoved it in a drawer somewhere. It's actually quite pretty.

Chana: How do you feel when you aren't loving yourself?

Linda: It really hurts. I blame my mom for not loving me, but even when she gives me love, I come up with some story about how she's just trying to manipulate me. That's so sad.

Chana: So how would you like to treat yourself?

Linda: Lovingly. I want to love myself.

Chana: What is some **Action** that you can take to get that going?

Linda: First off, I can take a bath tonight instead of a shower. If I don't watch that stupid cop show, I can easily make the time. I can do that every week. Wow.

Chana: Why did you say, "Wow?"

Linda: I feel good. I thought getting love would be so difficult, that I'd have to work hard for it, but taking a bath is so easy, and it goes a long way.

Chana: What else would you like to do?

Linda: Go to bed earlier. But how?

Chana: How do you think?

Linda: This is embarrassing. My kids are teens already. They can fold their own laundry and prep their own lunches for school. I guess if they did that they'd be loving me more. And probably loving themselves more because they'd get to pick what they eat rather than nag me about what they don't like.

Chana: Why'd you smile?

Linda: This is great. I'm doing *less* and feeling *better*. It's revolutionary! Okay. What else can I do?

Chana: What's your answer to your question?

Linda: I can wear Mom's jewelry. The few times I've worn a piece, I've gotten tons of compliments on it. Just imagining myself wearing the pearl necklace she got me for my 30th feels good. It's like I'd be enveloped by her love all day. Hmm.

Chana: Why did you say that?

Linda: It just occurred to me how much time and thought and effort Mom probably puts into buying me gifts. I bet every year she tries even harder, hoping that *this time*, I'll be happy with what she gives me. Another thing I can do is wear them, thank her, and tell her about the compliments I get. I bet she'd feel loved by that, too.

Chana: I'd like you to close your eyes and imagine it's tomorrow. Your kids are now responsible for their laundry and school lunches, you've taken a long bubble bath, and you're wearing the pearl necklace. How do you feel?

Linda: I feel warm inside, full of light, excited for the day. The biggest thing is that I feel grateful for the people in my life. It's good.

Chana: What thoughts, if any, come to you?

Linda: It's not a thought so much, more a feeling. I feel warm and just… *good* inside. I feel loving. I like everyone more. Life is okay; I'm okay. If I could put it into words, it would be, "I love you."

As a product of engaging in loving behaviors, Linda created a **Tower of Benefit** filled with thoughts of love and acceptance. Becoming an **Action Superhero** shaped how she saw herself and the world around her. Jefferson says we're defined by **Action** because we not only judge others by what they do, we assess our character, capabilities, and motives by our **Actions**. Building support for our beliefs is a great start, but what brings lasting peace and joy is acting in alignment with the truth.

You are an **Action Superhero** when you integrate the lessons that turnarounds teach you. Acting upon those lessons hammers them home and makes you a more honest, compassionate, and value-driven human being.

Download an **Action Superhero** worksheet from the **Free Bonus Section** of my website:

Hold.ChanaMason.com/bonus.

Afterword

Inquiry is a continuous process of exploring the thoughts that drive our feelings, physiology, and actions. The more time we allow ourselves to peel back the layers of unconscious beliefs, the more happy, peaceful, and loving our world will be.

I hope the tools this book help you in your healing process and assist you in helping others find their joy. I would love to hear about your experience using these tools or any tools you've collected yourself! Please drop me a line or two or twenty at **chanamason@gmail.com**.

I'd also like to take the time here to thank those who have been so monumental in my journey. Thanks to Joan and Chaya for deep soul healing. To Noga, Miriam, Batsheva, Nava, Leah, Chaya, Malta Sima, and Ayo for being my partners in crime. To Shimi, for your top-notch guidance. To Kaley and Rebecca for your feedback and sisterhood. To my clients (you know who you are) for blossoming so beautifully before my eyes and for mirroring the lessons I need to learn. To the Holy One, for blessing my life even when I'm not grateful. And to Dave and Aryeh Lev for your endless patience, love, and confidence.

Bibliography

Byron Katie offers many resources, from recordings of dozens of dialogues to worksheets, books, and live courses on her website **TheWork.com**.

Noga Hullman is a close friend and mentor. She first introduced me to Byron Katie and has been an enormous resource of ideas and support with this book. She helps mothers find peace of mind and personal growth in every parenting situation. Check her out at **NogaHullman.com**

Eckhart Tolle's books and talks have the elegant power to elevate your consciousness just by being in the presence of his words. You can find lectures, books, and other resources at **www.eckharttolle.com**.

Sydney Banks is a Scottish philosopher who created a process of disentanglement with our erroneous thinking called *The Three Principles*. Watch and learn at **SydBanks.com**.

T Harv Eker's book *Secrets of the Millionaire Mind* helps people rework their thinking around money and success.

Stephen Covey's *7 Habits of Highly Effective People* is often referenced in my home when we're considering how we want to treat each other and engage with the world at large.

Barry Neil Kaufman's *Option Process* requires a bit of work to learn but is well worth it. Reading *To Love is to Be Happy With* is a great place to start. To get a taste of his dialogues, I recommend reading *Giant Steps*, which you can find on his website **Option.org**.

Made in the USA
Middletown, DE
10 May 2019